10/9

Martin Wainwright

gb

Published by Guardian Books 2009

Copyright © Martin Wainwright 2009

First published in Great Britain in 2009 by

Guardian Books
Kings Place, 90 York Way
London N1 9GU

www.guardianbooks.co.uk

A CIP catalogue record for this book
is available from the British Library

ISBN 978-0-85265-113-1

Designed and typeset by Two Associates

Printed and bound in Great Britain by Clays Ltd, St Ives PLC

To Guardian *colleagues*
in Manchester – past, present and future

Contents

Introduction

'... in the north long since, my nest was made.'
Alfred, Lord Tennyson, *The Princess*

When I was a teenager I noticed a book on the shelves of Headingley library in Leeds called *South*, and for some perverse reason I took it out. I got a surprise. Instead of an analysis of the soft world of the home counties and jessiedom generally, it was about tough, taciturn men doing gritty things in a landscape of rock and ice. The cover showed fields of snow and a spiky ridge above wild water which looked even worse than Sharp Edge seen from the Glendcramackin valley in the Lake District.

Something was wrong; a misfile by the waspish woman who stamped our books, or another of her shelving errors? No, this was indeed the south, as far south as you can go: Antarctica, as seen through the eyes of Sir Ernest Shackleton in 1919.

The episode was a lesson in the multiple meanings of simple words and the way that failure to understand this leads to misconceptions. Another of my mistakes has been the cherished belief that my birth in Leeds unquestionably qualifies me as a northerner. Rubbish, say friends in Newcastle upon Tyne, who reckon Leeds and Manchester to be in the Midlands (partly, admittedly, to wind up Lancastrians

or Yorkshiremen such as myself). But then I belatedly discovered the joys of Philip Pullman's marvellous book *Northern Lights* and found that his north is Spitzbergen, or Svalbard, where Geordies will certainly be considered Midlanders in their turn.

Where you draw the north-south border will never be resolved, I fear, but that's no bad thing as debating the matter makes for a good parlour game or discussion in the pub. I thought we might get agreement when neutral naturalists suggested the southernmost habitats of the great hairy northern ant, which roughly coincide with my personal belief that the north embraces everything in England down to the river Trent. But then someone counter-attacked with the northern limits of the Southern Wainscot moth, which would extend the south's empire almost to Cumbria.

Amid these subtleties, jests and flexible usages, however, one image has been shockingly immune to change: the notion of the north of England as seen from the south, and especially from London. It has remained constant during my 22 years of working in the north for the *Guardian*, the last 13 of them as northern editor. I have written and broadcast a lot about it, and for most of that time, the fantastic misconceptions have not really bothered me. Those of us who live in the north know the pleasant, relaxed and friendly reality of life here. I cannot count the number of times I have been told: 'Stop saying how nice it is, else they'll all want to come and spoil it.' I remember fondly a job at Linton Colliery in Northumberland where locals were quietly pleased that the village had actually been removed from the Ordnance Survey. The mapmakers failed to realise that there was a village as well as the actual colliery, and rubbed them both out when the pit closed.

But during my time I have also seen two developing trends, one good, one bad and both related to image as well as reality. The promotion of a 'new north' has attracted newcomers and outsiders to settle, with invaluable effects on the energy and prosperity of all of us up here. At the same time, the centrifugal force of modern Britain has quickened the spiral of talent, power and influence down to London. It has sucked colleague after colleague out of my own working life without replacement, so that my august job title is now perilously close to becoming a fiction.

So it seems a good time to set my thoughts down, although certainly not as a last will and testament. There are three central themes to my discussion and they are all positive. I want to set out the virtues of the north, to encourage my fellow northerners to be equally upbeat about them and to put outsiders' clichés into their proper place as ever such unoriginal fun.

I am sorry that you will often encounter the pronoun 'I' in the process, but we are told to practise what we preach and my sermon is the result of experience. I had an idyllic childhood in the north and its glow was not reduced when I was sent away to school in Herefordshire and then Shropshire for almost half my life between the ages of seven and 18. On the contrary, I learned to appreciate other parts of England and to understand that to praise the north is not to denigrate anywhere else, including London which I was intensely excited to visit for the first time at the age of 16 and which I love and consider to be my capital as much as any Cockney's. It seemed right, too, that north London was at the time considered a cut above the capital's own south.

I then returned north with my wife, Penny, and had the pleasure of helping to bring up children in Leeds, which was on the up throughout their formative years. Both of us have also been given the chance to work with lively, upbeat colleagues, Penny in her writing for *Yorkshire Life* and as a trustee first of the Thackray Museum in

Leeds – the country's national medical museum in all but name – and now of the Hepworth in Wakefield which opens in 2011 in honour of the city's famous sculptor. I have had the *Guardian* crew plus a stimulating spell as first chair of the National Lottery charities board in Yorkshire and the Humber. That was a robust northern group which pioneered reforms in grant-making, open meetings and more public involvement in the process. We were so cheerful and persuasive that the rest of the country followed suit, and when I was given the MBE on the committee's behalf, the Queen seemed to sense the buzz, and smiled broadly as I told her in my statutory half-minute how excellently things were going off in Barnsley.

I don't need telling that life isn't lovely for everyone. My upbringing and the whole of my working life since 1987 have taken me into plenty of the north's bad places, but you hardly need another misery memoir about them. Unless you live on Mars or lead a life untroubled by newspapers, radio or television, you will have had the north presented to you in terms of little else. That is the lop-sided version I would like to try to begin to correct. I have also lived on a settlement in east London, which has the country's poorest council wards, and I can take you to Bath – yes, even exquisite Bath – and show you some sorry places indeed. In all three, the Georgian gem, the mighty capital and our vast and magnificent region, they are a part of the picture. In none of them, the whole.

So no, it wasn't and it isn't grim up north, to use for the one and only time that dreadful cliché of headline-writers. At the *Guardian's* office in Manchester we have trained a succession of young colleagues from London who almost all left wistfully, warmed by the quality of life and relative lack of stress. I have never met a southern student who has failed to enjoy Leeds, Manchester, Newcastle or Sheffield. Penny's colleagues at the Thackray included the then director of the British Museum, Dr Robert Anderson, who could be lionised at London salons but was only too keen to bound on to a train at King's Cross. In the elderly and disabled people's lunch club where she helps there are Cockneys happily resettled and Belgians and Italians too. And as a family, constantly urging people to come and stay and see for themselves, we have found that southern and London friends who take up the invitation invariably agree. Some have even moved here.

I apologise for some terrible gaps. I was born lacking a basic human gene which has left me without any interest in sport. A paean to the north could be made up of little else and, for normal people, a list of reasons for living here might be topped by proximity to Old Trafford, Anfield or St James's Park. Likewise, I am cloth-eared and out of date on modern music. I was listening only this morning – April 2009 – to a clip on Radio 5 about a group called Doves of whom I had never heard. But I became an instant fan of them, when their singer Jimi Goodwin, who met the other members of the band at Wilmslow High school, told the interviewer that none of them were into what he called 'northern miserablism.' Seeking more information after this promising start, I found a review by my colleague Alexis Petridis which said of one of their northern songs:

'The landscape of Lancashire is depicted with the grand romanticism songwriters usually reserve for America. "The road back to Preston was covered all in snow," they sing, sounding not bathetic or knowing, but rather awestruck at the sight.'

Those are my boys! I am a Doves fan for life.

So much for my individual context. To collectivise it, I have raided mercilessly a very large collection of northern books, magazines and pamphlets which I have built up over two decades, along with some 10,000 articles written for the *Guardian* since 1987. About a third of these were only ever seen by myself, a succession of copytasters and God, but the others are available online. I owe warm acknowledgements and warm thanks to all the other authors; to save space, paper and trees, I am compiling a full bibliography on *http://martinwainwright-truenorth. blogspot.com* where I would greatly welcome comments, debate and corrections (I am, remember, a journalist…)

I must, however, thank Lisa Darnell of Guardian Books here, and her colleagues Helen Brooks and Sara Montgomery; it is always a pleasure to work with them. Ditto Nick Downing and my tireless wife Penny who read the proofs. As always, Penny was full of encouragement and patience plus restraint when I got over-excited about the north's charms. Many thanks also to Cameron Fitch of Two Associates for the book's appropriately cheerful design, and especially my long-standing colleague Michael McNay who read the original draft and suggested many and excellent changes to keep my argument from wandering on to mantraps and thin ice. I have adopted almost all of them, but if I still fall into, or through, any oubliettes then I am responsible and I apologise.

Finally, I am really honoured to have so many pictures in the book by my companions on *Guardian* jobs for many years, the late Don McPhee, Denis Thorpe and Chris Thomond. Don's exhibition The View From Manchester at Manchester Art Gallery in 2005 broke attendance records and the Lowry was thronged daily in 2008 for A Long Exposure, curated by Denis and featuring the work of all three. Chris still roams the north with me and there could be no better colleague or more imaginative source of ideas. Mariam Yamin, the *Guardian's* archivist, gave her usual unstinting help with finding photographs, and I would specially like to thank Eric Hilaire of the *Guardian* picture desk for his tireless part in the picture selection. On the strength of the well-known adage, the pictures which he has so carefully chosen add 125,000 words.

1

The Glorious Burden

*'Manchester now hurls back upon her detractors the
charge that she is too deeply absorbed in the pursuit of
material wealth to devote her energies to the finer arts.'*
Illustrated London News 1857

The north is both our glory and our problem. It is the land that
gave birth to all the clichés – dark, grim, cobbled and the rest of
it – because in its heyday they were true. No part of England has had
a stronger character, and you do not part with that sort of reputation
easily. Huge mills, smoking chimneys, mass workforces; they were all
there and sometimes you think, despairingly, that they will cling on
indelibly for ever. Everything in the north was very big, everywhere,
and in the towns and cities, it was very black.

Soot actually fell visibly at times, like a thinly gentle form of snow,
and this was in my lifetime (59 years now), quite apart from the
testimony of long ago. When I wrote a mini-thesis on a Victorian
election in Leeds for my undergraduate degree, I proudly announced
that even in 1971, 25 tons of soot fell every month on every square
mile of the city south of the river Aire. I don't know if you can

Old north incarnate. Manchester in 1962

imagine 25 tons of soot in a heap, but plenty of north-watchers have done. There is an unbroken trail of the stuff from Lady Marney in Disraeli's *Sybil*: 'You never have a clear sky. Your toilette table is covered in blacks [soot scraps]; the deer in the park seem as if they had bathed in a lake of Indian ink; and as for the sheep, you expect to see chimney sweeps for the shepherds'; through JB Priestley's *English Journey* describing Manchester in 1934: 'The real city sprawls all over south Lancashire. It is an Amazonian jungle of blackened bricks'; to my Auntie Barbara: 'When we moved to Leeds from Somerset in the 1950s, Marty, I'd only to leave washing out for more than half an hour and the smuts'd have it dirtier than before.' Had I heard of

Mrs Gaskell at the time, I would have replied: 'Count yourself lucky, Auntie. Mrs Gaskell's wouldn't stay clean for more than a week in Manchester – and that's when they were hung indoors.'

Still, as everyone said, it was good for the roses (by choking the aphids and blanketing blackspot with a black carpet which killed the bacteria and could then be brushed off). And that stout-hearted reaction was more northern than the soot in the end. The north wasn't a grim place when I was a boy. Read the ebullient recollections of Alan Bennett and Keith Waterhouse, and before them JB Priestley, and you find a delight and relish about the size and solidity of everything, from Manchester town hall to Philip Smith's legendary Bradford pies. Priestley's radio talk about Smith's shop in Ivegate during the war has been held up rightly as a model way of sustaining civilian morale. It reminded listeners that as well as defending democracy and other long words, the nation was fighting for its pastry and that lovely meat jelly which liquefies when warmed. You mustn't tilt a hot pie when carrying it home.

Blackness made northerners happy too. Even if it wasn't exclusive to the north, it was reckoned to be inkier or even more velvet than anyone else's noir. I was intrigued when I went to beautiful Bath as a young reporter to see how black the honey-coloured stone had become there, on sides of the streets which took the muck from fires on the prevailing wind. But did that wash, as it were, with my new colleagues in the north when I returned there? Heck no! The urban landscape of the northern cities was on an altogether vaster scale, and within it were individually massive canvases for soot, such as town halls, which would have put whole sections of Bath in the shade. When a bus clipped a chunk of stone off Dewsbury town hall in the early 1960s, the replacement had to be sprayed so that it would fit in with the rest of the sooty building. I am old enough to remember

Leeds town hall in its truly black livery before it was cleaned to reveal the subtle colours we see today.

That change was much too subtle for some. Phil Sidey, the first manager of Radio Leeds, ran a Clean Leeds Town Hall campaign in the late 1960s and was summoned to lunch as a result by the then leader of the city council, Frank Marshall, a strong-minded character who was later made a Conservative peer. 'We like it as it is,' Marshall told Sidey, and when the cheeky reply came, 'Well, perhaps that's why so many young people leave Leeds,' the temperature fell by degrees. Bonhomie was only restored when Sidey cast around for some mollifying banality and came up with: 'Yorkshire fish and chips are the best in the world, aren't they?' That broke the silence, but his attack on the black town hall was not forgotten, although he was right. I was involved recently in the rediscovery of a film about Leeds by Sir John Betjeman which was made in 1968 but got lost in a squabble between the BBC TV's offices in the city and Manchester, with their London HQ not bothered about whether it got shown by either. It didn't, until early 2009, and my first reaction when I watched it was: why ever did they bother to use colour film? Everything was so dark. It is no surprise that the names of two famous puppets invented in Guiseley on the edge of Leeds, which took children's television by storm in the 1950s, were Sooty and Sweep.

The soot came from something that fostered real and justifiable pride: manufacturing. Perhaps fondness for muck was transferred from the north's more understandable delight in its ability to make things, be they pies or steam engines. A northerner, Sir George Cayley, was the first man to build an (unpowered) aeroplane that flew. Another, Joseph Priestley, discovered the main component of the air it flew in. A third, John Harrison, used wonderfully inventive design, including a wood that bled sap so slowly that it oiled itself, to invent the chronometer that allowed ships – and in due course aeroplanes – to know where they were. All this was boastfully flaunted, and much, much more, even in fields that would normally be discussed *sotto voce* or, in the south of the day, never at all. When Bradford corporation got fed up with griping letters from the Stansfield family of Esholt Hall about the polluted state of the river Aire, which semi-circled their croquet lawn, it compulsorily purchased the whole estate and built Europe's largest sewage works there. Uniquely in the world of waste, huge pressing mills were installed in stone buildings with Greek porticos which looked as though they would last 1,000 years. Above each was the Bradford motto: *Labor omnia vincit.*

What work was conquering in this titanic setting was the immense amount of lanolin in Bradford's wool waste, which gushed from the plant's 128 steam presses and was sold in aid of municipal funds to

No soot now in Hebden Bridge, West Yorkshire

Halifax 1966. The end of its grimy prime

manufacturers of soap and cosmetics. By 1949 it had realised £3 million in profits (£800 million at 2009 prices) and, together with sales of the remaining sludge to farmers as fertiliser, was still meeting all Esholt's costs every year. One of the neatest links the north was later to establish between its past and present was the use of Esholt village, where the sewage workers lived, as the setting for Yorkshire TV's *Emmerdale*. Sewage soap gave way to TV soap, and many were the comparisons made.

The rest of Esholt works was meanwhile on a similarly magnificent scale. The three-mile main outfall tunnel from Bradford was wide enough to take cars and on the grand opening day in 1923, the Lord Mayor and corporation duly processed through in a succession of locally made Jowetts. As the lead car appeared out of the gloom, the civic architect's wife turned to her husband and said, without trying to lower her voice: 'Here comes the first load of shit.'

Even today, with columbine twining round the old stones as waste is burned in a modern plant nearby (and recycled into breeze blocks for the house-building trade), Esholt looks northern in the traditional sense. But it was certainly never seen as grim, because its work was so obviously an improvement on what had gone on before. The same applied to the north's great housing estates and especially the grey rendered, eight-storey barracks of Quarry Hill flats in central Leeds. The fact which you will most often read or Google about them, is that Hitler thought them perfect for his putative northern headquarters – ie lowering and severe.

In fact, they were a stunning advance on the conditions their tenants had known before, when they were crammed in yards and alleys which only look pleasant – as they do today – when occupants squashed up to 10 in a bedroom are replaced by wine bars. 'They will be the finest flats for wage-earners in Europe,' said Alderman Blackah who chaired the housing committee in 1938. 'When the full scheme is completed, the public will be amazed at the beauty of it.' That day did not entirely come, because the second world war meant that extra facilities were skimped or abandoned, but the last tenants were sorry to leave when the 960 flats were demolished in 1978. Their structural flaws, a result of the wartime shortages and too much haste to re-house the slum dwellers, defeated a whole range of restoration plans – which variously included the idea (from Harwell laboratories) of 'atomic heating,' and painting the whole complex pastel pink. On the last day, naval signal flags were hoisted on the flats saying 'Goodbye world' after a plan to say 'Fuck off' was narrowly defeated. Quarry Hill put up with many insults in its time, but most epitaphs concluded that it was a noble, if flawed, experiment.

Massiveness applied, too, to the north's secular cathedrals where all this making of things went on: wool and cotton textiles, steel, coal, shipbuilding; the enormous industries which were the sinews of the three regions. One to take your breath away has been preserved at Magna, the science centre in Rotherham, housed in what was once the melting shop of Templeborough steel mills, which opened in 1917 to make artillery shells. Even today, the cavernous hall is the length of 10 football pitches, but there used to be more than twice as much of it; the cogging mills and cooling sheds have been demolished. Gone with them is the dark orange smog which often forced passing traffic to switch on headlights. You can get a better idea of such a titanic operation in action in certain places where large workforces still arrive and leave together in the manner of the mills emptying to the ring of clogs in the films of Gracie Fields. A good example, which you can combine with a lovely day in glorious countryside, is the early morning train from Barrow-in-Furness to Sellafield, three coaches or sometimes more crammed with yawning workers on their way to the British Nuclear Fuels plant. In winter, with the dark outside, men slumped with woollen hats pulled down and the carriages dimly lit and so fugged up that their windows stream with condensation, the general impression is of army recruits or merchant seamen going to enlist in 1939. The train seems of similar vintage, but at Sellafield station it empties almost completely. When I took it to start the first leg of the coast-to-coast walk early in the day, there was only me left plus an elderly woman and a schoolboy who, like me, asked the conductor to pull up at the next request stop, St Bees.

More often in recent years, such experiences have been a requiem; spending the last day of shipbuilding on the Wear discussing in disbelief with a work experience student, as we walked in 1988 past an apparently endless line of empty construction sheds and silent cranes, how so much equipment and investment could no longer be of any use. Similarly in York seven years later, when British Rail

Quarry Hill 1954. Grey but with space to play

engineering pulled out of the carriageworks where trains and rolling stock had been built for 112 years, the size of the newly-abandoned yards was hard to take in.

These experiences came to mind when I watched a marvellous series of films made by Sagar Mitchell and James Kenyon, who were great enthusiasts for the cine camera in the early 1900s. A hoard of their work was rediscovered in 1994 and restored over the next few years, bringing that period to life. Productions made and edited in the partners' home town of Blackburn show armies everywhere, men and women marching into the mills or docks at the beginning of shifts, out again at the end and off to chapel, parks and fairs en masse. They were armies in a uniform but not a military one, nearly everyone wearing clogs, the women in pinnies and shawls and the men all with the same, or very similar, flat caps.

The flat cap is of course one of the really tenacious legacies of the north, although they haven't even been made here for a decade. When production moved in 2000 from the last British flat cap factory, JW Myers of Leeds, to Panyu in China, the cap had also morphed into niche fashion wear thanks to the rappers and Samuel L Jackson in the Quentin Tarantino film *Jackie Brown*. But there is another reason for the persistent belief that they are still worn: the iconic northern working man is much more than a regional caricature; he is a mighty global icon. The most famous individual example, the Daily Mirror's cartoon character Andy Capp, is a perfect illustration of this.

He was sent to the paper in 1957 by his creator Reg Smythe, a man who lived in his native Hartlepool until his death in 1998, in response to an advertisement for a strip cartoon to be published in the paper's northern edition only. As soon as the editor Hugh Cudlipp saw the work, he realised that Smythe had created an everyman who would be loved (and hated) all over Britain. Even this

Andy Capps. Northern but universal too

was an underestimate. Capp is published in more than 50 countries where his counterpart is to be found, south, north, east and west. In the Netherlands they call him Jan met de Pet, in Ghana, An'Dicap. The editor of an Ankara newspaper which serialised him says simply: 'Andy is the most Turkish fellow I ever met.'

Just as Andy transcended a simple 'northern' image, so the workplaces of the north's armies were much more complicated and specialised than they looked; textiles covered an enormous variety of processes as well as materials: carding, spinning, felt-making from shoddy, the scrag end left from superior cloths which was also known as mungo because the overlookers at the worsted or woollen mills dismissed it as inferior stuff which 'mun' – must – go. The generalised term 'steel city' for Sheffield included everything from teaspoons to entire battleships which representatives of foreign powers could, and did, order on a day visit from their embassies via the railway line from St Pancras. Each product was likely to require half-a-dozen or more separate metalworking skills. The simplistically-termed 'coalfields' similarly produced a long list of different types of fuel, suitable for home fires, power stations, steel furnaces and the boilers of railway locomotives and steam ships.

These industries brought employment on a previously unimaginable scale, and created wealth which was similarly unprecedented, outside the palaces of royalty. Louis Crossley of the Halifax carpet dynasty toured his grounds at Moorside on a small electric tramway and installed an organ indoors which the admiring *Halifax Courier* described as 'a huge instrument, somewhat similar to the great organ in the Royal Albert Hall.' Sir Isaac Holden, another textile baron who was also a Liberal MP and one of the richest men in the country, installed such a complicated heating system in his vast palace at Oakworth, with 36,500 feet of four-inch cast-iron pipes, that the place burnt down. The ghostly outline of his extraordinary orchid house is now a small park which includes the vanished mansion's portico with its inaccurate motto: *Extant recte factis praemia*. The rewards of good deeds endure. Not any more they don't, in Oakworth.

Like their workforce and their products, these men were seldom the cliché bosses of dramas based in the north, which were deftly satirised by the TV comedy *Brass* with its ruthless Bradley Hardacre forever pitted against the poor but honest Fairchild family who slaved for him. In reality manufacturing required them to have a sensitivity to new developments and design. This was especially the case with textiles, where commercial success went hand in hand with artistic flair, as *Brass* acknowledged, through Hardacre's aesthetic gay son Maurice. Engineering was the same, demanding exact measurements and the imagination to find new materials, such as the dense plastic of Sir John Charnley's hip joints at Wrightington hospital near Wigan or new ways of overcoming problems of gearing or traction. The Kitson family, which made railway engines in Leeds, was a case in point.

Kitson locomotives can still be found hauling trains on the world's highest railways in the Andes, or closer to home, but still impressive enough, on the Snowdon Mountain Railway. Two 20th century descendants, the brothers Sydney and Robert Kitson, became respectively experts on John Sell Cotman and Sir Frank Brangwyn. Sydney wrote Cotman's biography and amassed Britain's biggest private collection of the painter's watercolours, bequeathing much of it to Leeds on his death in 1937. Robert made a similar public gift, the wonderful mosaics installed by Brangwyn in St Aidan's church on Roundhay Road in Leeds. Originally intended to be a painted mural, the huge scenes of four periods from the saint's life in the north were done with tesserae after the artist convinced his patron

Weaving worsted cloth in Huddersfield

that a painting would be ruined within a few years, by soot. Kitson also commissioned Brangwyn to decorate his villa in Taormina, Sicily, the Casa Cuseni, an Arts and Crafts house which he designed himself. He was a generous and popular citizen in the town, whose people conspired together to hide his valuables during the war, when he had to return to Britain in a hurry to avoid internment. As soon as the Nazi occupiers had been driven out, they asked him to return and elected him Taormina's mayor.

Such broad interests were not the monopoly of the north's wealthy. Mrs Gaskell noted the enthusiasm for knowledge of Manchester factory workers, for whom the *Manchester Guardian* organised one of the newspaper world's first cut-price subscriptions based on class. She fictionalised it in *Mary Barton*, writing: 'There are a class of men in Manchester and all the manufacturing districts of Lancashire who know the name and habitat of every plant within a day's walk of

The drama of steel at Firth Brown, Sheffield

their dwellings.' A real-life example, a textile worker called Robert Cribb, did the city a good turn in 1829 by discovering an insect now known as the Manchester moth on Kersal Moor in central Salford, a wildish, Hampstead Heath-like green lung. He captured some 50 of the yellow and brown species, scientifically known as *Schiffermulleria woodiella*, but got into an argument over rent with his landlady, who burned his insect collection. Only three Manchester moths were salvaged but as none has ever been caught since, this has given the species the distinction of being among the rarest moths in the world. When the story was retold at a meeting of the Royal Entomological Society in Manchester in 1951, a *Manchester Guardian* leader noted: 'We are not cotton-spinners all, sang Tennyson. But he might have been a bit more respectful about these parts if he had known about our eminent moth.'

In the same way, preconceptions were often shattered when you met figures like the long-serving leader of Durham county council in the 1980s. The authority was rock-solid Labour of course and Mick Terrans was a miner who went down the pit at the age of 14. But that was the only predictable part of the story. At the age of 12, Terrans had showed an entrepreneurial spirit that Norman Tebbit would have applauded, getting on his bike to go to local hairdressers where he taught himself enough to cut his friends' hair for a few pennies. Within the year, he was working two evenings a week in the barbers at Trimdon, later the constituency home of Tony Blair, although the future prime minister arrived too late to have a trim from Mick. Before Terrans was 13, he was earning 7s 6d for these stints which was only 9d less than he got as an apprentice underground. Once up from the pit and in the fresh air again, he was soon supplementing his wage as a part-time, self-employed bookie. Talk to Terrans for a while and you found out more and more. He was a very keen Anglican and turned his council skills to good account on the parochial church council, the Sedgefield deanery synod and the Durham diocesan conference, where he found a good intellectual sparring partner in the radical bishop, David Jenkins. At 81 he made a parachute jump in aid of research into Alzheimer's disease.

In the boardroom and at the coalface alike, everyone benefited from the good times, but the enormous size of the north's heavy industry and related institutions gave a false impression of permanence. Consider that last word in one of its best-known northern contexts, the Leeds Permanent building society which has proved anything but permanent. It has gone, like the Yorkshire Penny Bank where you could once indeed start an account with one (old) penny, and this disappearance would have been hard to imagine in the heyday of the north. My grandfather on my mother's side was chairman of the

Leeds Permanent in the 1940s and it was the family's belief that he had suggested its motto, down-to-earth and resolutely not in Latin: Safe and Sound. So it seemed, and so it might have remained if mutual status had not been vulnerable to the temptations of bonuses, share allocations and the other glittering attractions – in 1997 – of becoming a bank.

Prosperity seldom endures. The achilles heel of the north's vast industries was that a fall in their fortunes was as concentrated in its effects as success had been. Business failure could virtually close a factory town down. The titans created a dependency, psychological as well as physical, and it was disastrous when they entered hard times. Even today, promoters of remaining, dominant industries like the nuclear complex in Cumbria have this at the back of their minds. When financial disaster struck in the 1930s, there entered, too, another familiar image of the north: strikers, queues of the unemployed, marches on London from Jarrow and many less well-remembered departure points on other occasions. The phenomenon, with its one-out, all-out atmosphere, ranged from huge affairs to a lilliputian action I covered in 1994, involving the entire membership of the Card Setting Machine Tenters Union. That involved only 40 people but half of them, including the general secretary, had been sacked by a company in Brighouse which couldn't afford to pay for their skill at making cards with metal spikes to comb rubbish from fleeces, when there were cheap imports including mass-produced teasel heads, with their ingeniously hooked thorns.

The embrace of virtually entire areas by a single industry had another effect which survived both good and bad times: the creation of strong communities with roots which have passed into northern lore and and are not yet dead. There is nowhere a Dewsbury man or woman disdains more strongly than Batley, a mile to the north. A

Shipyard workers at Barrow-in-Furness

loyalist of Rawdon, where I live, will have nothing good to say about Yeadon, just up the hill, or Guiseley, the next community along the A65. London? An abomination certainly, but far away and not a clear and present danger like them next door.

This suspicion is part of the glue that binds a community together, but that is not necessarily a virtuous or appealing characteristic. The word 'community' is too lazily used nowadays as if it were always a source of universal joy. In practice, a strong community may be nothing more than a selfish, warm huddle or degenerate into a defensive ghetto, hideously exemplified by gated communities. More of that later because it has not only existed in the past up here but still does. But it was never the dominant northern way.

There was a well-documented caution towards outsiders, the 'off-cummed uns' of legend who are more usually called 'comers-in.' But with this went a recognition that new energy and different ways of seeing things revitalised community and especially economic life. It was Scots who built up the marketing system that turned Bradford into 'Woolopolis', the world entrepôt of that part of the textile trade. It was Armenians who played a pivotal part in Manchester's early 20th century commercial revival, an influx of newcomers fleeing the Turkish massacres at a providential time for the north.

In turn, this acknowledgment of outsiders, however grudging at times, attracted others who found the north fascinating in its own terms. A notable example of this type was Nigel Morgan who died in 2006 on holiday in Croatia, but at the age of 70 after a long and productive life. He was a man of Kent who initially had no connection with the north at all. A clever young Cambridge graduate, he went out with the 60s' favourite comedienne Eleanor Bron, who made her name on the satirical TV programme *That Was the Week That Was*. At the same time, Morgan was part of the group behind the foundation of *Private Eye*, another powerful pin in the establishment's behind. He pored over proofs with Richard Ingrams, Willie Rushton and Christopher Booker. And then he suddenly decided to go and teach history at the grammar school in Preston.

This was the north's gain, mightily. Morgan became a remarkable expert on local history. He published a book on the housing of the old handloom weavers called *Vanished Dwellings* and then followed it up with another on the slums of the Industrial Revolution which he called *Deadly Dwellings*. He moved to St Martin's College in Lancaster and then back to Preston on the foundation of the University of Central Lancashire, and became one of Britain's foremost experts on the history of social housing. Why? It was down to his two years' national service as an RAF Vampire jet pilot before Cambridge, which left him two legacies. One was the feeling, common among older students, that a lot of undergraduate life was glitzy but trivial,

Clocking on at Birkenhead shipyard, 1972

a criticism which he later applied to the swinging London of the 1960s. The other was a fascination with the Vampire. It was a classic piece of northern manufacturing by English Electric in Preston.

Part of the attraction of the north for a man like Morgan was the down-to-earth nature of a society which made this complex machine, but still had time and energy to maintain a co-operative, neighbourly community in the streets around the aircraft factory. I encountered this for myself when I went to Preston in 2008 to report on the effects of the latest contraction of Britain's aircraft industry; in the community hall opposite the gates of the huge BAE plant, as it had now become, people with learning difficulties were enjoying a lunch club, with drama lessons afterwards.

Such a society also accounts, I am sure, for the popularity of the autobiographical account of a northern childhood by the academic William Woodruff, *The Road to Nab End*. This could have been another

Manchester from the Guardian *office 1951*

of today's cult of 'misery lit' descriptions of a dreadful upbringing, because before Woodruff escaped and soared through the 'socialist college', Plater at Oxford, his lot was tough indeed. His family were cotton mill workers and defenceless from the 1930s depression. His grandmother Bridget, who gave him the priceless gift of loving books – any book, all books – ended her life in Blackburn workhouse.

Woodruff, a friend of Harold Wilson's at Oxford and a better public speaker than the future prime minister, acknowledges all this. He describes how foolish speculation in London and Wall Street destroyed neighbourly co-operative societies such as his family's in Blackburn, which had no fallback when textile company loans were abruptly called in by the banks. But *The Road to Nab End* – originally called *Billy Boy* until someone in Little, Brown's syndication department pointed out that this was the name of Germany's most popular condom – was not just about that. It told the story of an

Getting cleaner. Manchester in 1984

Slump. Barrow shipbuilders queue for jobs

irrepressible, optimistic boy who took his grandma's advice to heart. Schooled on a Lifebuoy Soap encyclopaedia, he wrote to the Soviet embassy in the 1920s, asking for a job in the new workers' paradise. When he got no reply, he tramped his way to London, worked in a foundry and fell in with Labour party activists who saw his potential and got him to Oxford.

Caring and sharing within a village, town or workplace, of the sort immortalised by Woodruff, went with a belief in making things better – for everyone. That was a crucial (but subsequently overlooked) part of the self-improvement gospel of that sturdy northerner Samuel Smiles. Self might come first, but once a man or woman's reasonable needs and those of their family were met, it was on to neighbours and in so far as practical, the rest of the world. This is not an exclusively northern trait of course, but it was very strong here. Methodism, liberalism, socialism and, yes, even the Anglican toryism of reformers such as Richard Oastler saw to that. I will even call Margaret Thatcher as a witness, through her notorious but misrepresented comment that there is no such thing as society. Here is the transcript of her interviewer, Douglas Keay's recording for *Woman's Own*: 'There is no such thing as society. There is living tapestry of men and women and people and the beauty of that tapestry and the quality of our lives will depend upon how much each of us is prepared to take responsibility for ourselves and each of us prepared to turn round and help by our own efforts those who are unfortunate.' And again, in the same interview: 'Who is society? There is no such thing! There are individual men and women and there are families and no government can do anything except through people and people look to themselves first. It is our duty to look after ourselves and then also to help look after our neighbour.' In other words, society isn't a separate entity which will look after us; it is us. Mrs Thatcher was from Grantham, which is not the north, but she had a Methodist father from a hard-working background and the Trent isn't a long way north-east of her town. No wonder that through Parliamentary footsoldiers such as Elizabeth Peacock, daughter of a Skipton millworker, Sir Donald Thompson, son of a butcher, or Sir Marcus Fox, grammar school boy and Woolworth's salesman, she had – still has – plenty of enthusiasts up here.

With this communal muscle and sense of energy and progress, whatever the church or party banner floating over it, victories on suffrage, employment conditions and social reform were very often powered from the north: the Chartists' great newspaper was the *Northern Star*, the Independent Labour Party was founded in Bradford, the suffragette Pankhursts were Mancunians. Such a concentration of radical causes was also partly owing to the way that the north suffered disproportionately from industrial evils and political exclusion, and there was a further cause. Like the developing 'new north' to which we will turn shortly, the traditional one was a stronghold of exceptional vigour.

It inherited the virtues of independence, ravishing surroundings and an arm's length from London – but stamped its own mark upon them. The energy with which it built on these foundations was unparalleled in English history before the 19th century. Some of the building was literal. The new mills of the Industrial Revolution were often in previously out-of-the-way places such as the upper valleys of the Pennines, because that was where water power could be tapped, as well as flocks of sheep easily corralled to provide wool. Hence those precarious urban landscapes so iconic of the north, such as Hebden Bridge with its flying freeholds, back-to-backs turned into ups-and-downs because the hillsides are so steep. Parliament passed a special law to give the owners of the 'ups' freehold rights in spite of the fact that another dwelling, the 'down', is below theirs. Hence the 'flying'.

But the more fundamental sort of building was metaphorical and its dynamo was optimism. In any period after the initial, early 19th century onslaught of the factory system, the essential fact was that life was improving, all the time. A stupendous change was taking place; in 1851, agriculture was still Britain's biggest employer, a crown it had worn since the concept of a job began. But the 1,790,000 people working on the land – all over the country – were only just ahead of textiles, which employed 1,650,000, most of them in the north. By the 1901 census, farmworkers had shrunk to 689,300 and the heavy manufacturing sector was several million ahead.

During that half-century, manufacturing wages rose steadily most of the time, and during depressions their fall was eased by prices which dropped too. Greater wealth among working people, helped by imaginative schemes such as friendly societies and the co-operative

Liverpool docks before restoration

movement with its roots in the Pioneers of Toad Lane, Rochdale, increased the resources of the growing trade unions. Their influence, together with that of a bigger and more efficient civil service as the Government too became more wealthy, led to stricter regulation and better working conditions. You and I would not fling our caps in the air at the prospect of a 10-and-a-half-hour day and 60-hour week with Saturday afternoons off (church or chapel on Sunday), but in the 1870s that was a decided advance on what had gone before. Optimism and growing industrial clout marched together; an embryonic Trades Union Congress met for the first time in Manchester in 1868. The Workers' Education Association set up its first district in the north-west in 1904 and ran its first tutorial classes in Rochdale four years later. By 1914 it had 179 branches, most strongly represented in the north.

The children of the self-confident, late Victorian and Edwardian generation faced potentially disastrous reverses: the first world war and the depression, both on a scale that no one had foreseen or knew how to meet. But the upbringing of so many of those involved, in households which had known only a steady improvement in conditions, passed on the gene of positive thinking. There is nothing good to be said about the first world war. But the depression was faced in the north with defiance, imagination and by those who experienced the most dismal and long-lasting of its effects, perseverance. For evidence of this, you can still look around you today.

Come, for example, to Billingham on Teesside, which is currently referred to almost routinely as a 'toxic dump'. This is partly the fault, admittedly, of some local people whose understandable fears about pollution lead them to exaggerated descriptions which outsiders (Teesside, shudder) are happy to adopt, but this is a slur on the past. The arrival of ICI (at that time Brunner Mond) at Billingham in 1920 was the occasion for real excitement, as well as vision and pioneering spirit. Men like Amos Cowap, construction manager of what everyone was soon calling 'the Synthetic', were far-sighted and determined to bring better social conditions and steady employment as well as to make money. Garden estates are not a northern invention, but noble examples such as Dr Alfred Salter's in Bermondsey on the London Thames are minuscule compared with Cowap's housing for workers on Teesside, and many, many other similar places in the industrial north. Contemporary photographs in 1926, when the *Middlesbrough Evening Gazette* headlined 'Billingham's amazing growth' above a description of how the 'mushroom town has trebled population in four years', show new housing between Chilton's Lane and Milton Lane which looks as clean and smart as the private estates you see today on the greenfield rim of countless British towns.

There is a long catalogue of similar company initiatives in the north; the website Utopia Britannica has archived the best of such high-minded schemes. Here you will find the whoppers, such as Saltaire in West Yorkshire or Lord Lever's Port Sunlight on the tip of the Wirral. Beside them stands Vickerstown on Walney Island, off Barrow-in-Furness, with its 900 houses for shipbuilding workers, social institute, school, church and pub (denied to Saltaire by the teetotal Baptist Sir Titus Salt). And here too are Pilkington Glass's two garden suburbs at Ravenhead and Abercrombie in St Helen's. Or the high quality terraces built in Ashton under Lyne by the cotton manufacturer Hugh Mason, whose statue erected in the town by public subscription has been floodlit since March 2009 with the help of a grant from the Aksa Housing Association whose tenants now occupy many of the homes.

Similar principles governed non-commercial versions, such as the smallholding scheme which Lancashire Quakers established at the height of the depression in 1934 under the cumbersome title of the Wigan and District Subsistence Production Society. Workshops for cobblers, tailors and joiners were set up alongside allotments, and checks with the Inland Revenue and social security established that members – all unemployed – could take produce from both the smallholdings and workshops equivalent to the time they put in, without affecting their dole. The scheme flourished and expanded, adding on a 300-acre dairy farm, 54 acres of pigs, poultry and greenhouses, and a further 60 acres housing a bakery, jam-making and bacon-curing workshops.

Idealism as well as practicality remained the case when 'garden village' building was carried out on the massive scale you still see today in the Speke area of Liverpool, Wythenshawe in Manchester or Gipton, Middleton and Belle Isle in Leeds. These were not housing developments undertaken in a wholly functional spirit with expenditure the main claim on the designers' minds. There was a Messianic element too; an underlying purpose of realistically building anew. We are not talking satanic mills, but Chilton's Lane depended on the huge Brunner Mond buildings which stand in the background of the 1926 photos. Gipton needed Montagu Burton's tailoring works and the Royal Ordnance factory in Garforth.

A journey through the world of enlightened northern public works is absorbing and entertaining; one of my favourite regional landmarks is the very rare pissoir at Great Ayton, close to Captain Cook's birthplace above the Tees. The two circular metal booths joined in an S-shape are the only survivors of three similar structures which caused a minor constitutional stir when Great Ayton parish council had them installed on the French model in the late 1890s. The local drains had failed and problems were so persistent between 1898 and 1902 that the council took the matter into its own

Co-op divi stamps and tokens in Rochdale

hands, after complaints to more distant public heath authorities fell on uninterested ears in a way that would be familiar in the over-centralised world of today. The pissoirs were a great success, complete with metal signs saying Please Adjust Your Dress Before Leaving and warnings of 3d fines for loitering. It was then discovered, by one of the ratepayers' representatives who were sedulous about these things, that a parish council had no power to erect public lavatories. Great Ayton stuck to its guns, and won.

Several stories that I pursued in Bradford led me to discover a similar boldness in schools policy. On a sunny day in 1994 I queued with small pupils of Green Lane primary for a special dish of vegetarian aloo bonda to celebrate the imagination – and defiance of ratepayer councillors – of the school's headteacher 92 years earlier, Mr WH Sykes. Seriously concerned that some of his pupils were actually starving, during an acute recession, he brewed tea and bought jam and bread for them. This led to the introduction of Britain's first free school meals in 1902, which was promptly challenged and an argument raged until 1907, when the good guys won. Sykes and his colleagues went on to publish a recipe book for parents called *Shilling Meals for Seven*, which was reproduced for the anniversary. Before our aloo bonda, we had a starter from the book, lentil broth with small brown loaves. Very nice it was too, as well as luckily-suited to the British Asian pupils who by 1994 were in a majority at Green Lane.

Bradford also introduced the country's first swimming pool in a state school, and ran a marvellous open-air school in Buck Wood, Thackley, for consumptive children and others who were 'failing to thrive.' I interviewed half-a-dozen of these, by then robust octogenarians, for a radio programme and they told me how the classrooms' walls slid open to let in the healing fresh air, and on occasions the snow as well.

They were in my mind when I spoke some weeks later at a comprehensive school prizegiving in Rotherham. The strength of the

The post office, Port Sunlight

old north's images came up. The kids, with their online savvy and – at this particular school – an impressive track record in making films, were hacked off at the patronising ignorance of London and the south about their town and region. Some of them had just freshly encountered it at university interviews. Not so fast, I suggested; the proper reaction of a true northerner is to put anything and everything to practical and profitable use, including this. New northerners can don the old north mantle to their advantage, tucking the moth-eaten bits out of sight.

This is based on my own experience when I finished my indentures as an apprentice on the *Bath & Wilts Evening Chronicle* and applied, as all ambitious young journalists did, to the major titles in Fleet Street. I was given several interviews but it was clear from them, and from the letters of rejection, that a reporter who had spent three-and-a-half years in the supposed comfort and tranquillity of Bath would be under-equipped to cope with the real world. Less than a year later, I was doing the same round from the *Bradford Telegraph & Argus* and the reaction was entirely different. Bradford eh? Rippers, Black Panthers, woollen mills, trams (trolley buses, actually, and only the overhead pylons were left from them when I was there), moors, wuthering, restless immigrants ... Here's a young man who must know a thing or two. Give him a job. In fact, Bath was far more complex and often grittier than its image suggested, while life on the *T&A* had plenty of sunny interludes, including a look-on-the-bright-side initiative from the news editor which had me writing a weekly column called 'Happy People', one of the longest and most arduous series I have ever done. But harnessing the useful parts of old north is a characteristic of the world to which we now turn: the people of the new north.

2

Reinventing the North

'I cannot stand Andy Capp being used as a type of
northern man.'
Catherine Cookson

Tramp over the North York Moors until you come within sight of Whitby Abbey and the North Sea, and you descend into a network of beautiful valleys, green with sheep pasture in spring and tawny with dying bracken in the autumn. At the bottom of each, between quiet pools and tumbling waterfalls, run streams and by one of these, during boarding schools' long summer holidays, you might find a group of sketching teenage boys. Wander up within range of their chit-chat, and you realise that they are not local, although the chunky, grey-haired man advising them has the twang of the Tees. What have you stumbled across? A lesson being conducted by the head of the art department at Eton College, who lives just over the hill at Danby, a few miles from his birthplace in Redcar.

Ian Burke, the 13th master of drawing at Eton, is not the only teacher in the art department to commute on a weekly basis from

Lasting values. Tea beside Blackpool beach

Yorkshire and to live all the time at Danby during the holidays. Three others do too, and the landscape of the moors and coast is so important to them that in March 2009 they staged an exhibition of their work in Danby called Eton Beaks (the school's slang for 'teachers'). Burke is a good representative of the new north to start this chapter, because he bridges old and new. His own *alma mater* was a secondary modern in Redcar and an apprenticeship as a fitter at ICI, until a grandmother who admired his drawing skill intervened and got him to try for Sir William Turner's School, the local grammar. He made it, and then he was off, on the flight path of many talented young northerners. He got into Goldsmiths college in London. From the college, he got a job at Eton.

Burke made national headlines in 2005 when a member of his staff accused him of bullying her and in the messy legal aftermath suggested that he had given Prince Harry a hand towards the B grade in AS levels that was required to get officer training at Sandhurst. The bullying claim was upheld by an industrial tribunal, but not the royal allegations. Having met Burke and enjoyed a cup of tea and a long chat with him and his partner Susan Sharrard, herself an Eton art teacher, I suspect that he was simply plain-spoken rather than bullying, in the proper, insidious and undermining sense of the word. He certainly meets the requirements of any journalist looking for a traditional northerner, with his solid, stocky appearance, tales of working on North Sea rigs and fishing off the little port of Staithes. But his way of life and easy familiarity with a much wider world, and ability to put it to use, are new. On the walls of his studio hang two beautiful etchings of a Spanish hill village. 'My father loved Spain and retired there,' he explains. 'He bought two houses and left them to me. It was selling them which allowed me to buy this.' 'This' is a stunning converted mill by a beautiful stream.

Old man Burke was a pioneering northerner himself, by the sound of it. His savings came from hard, manual work on the rigs – traditional, tough, mega-scale work like the old north's – and when he went to Spain he adopted the ancient northern practice of buying your own house and the one next door (as a source of income, through rent). But that act of going to Spain, rather than Guisborough or Great Ayton, the pleasant outliers of Middlesbrough, was significant. It is part of the way that the excessive rootedness of northerners is breaking down.

Barry Rutter is another of these bridging characters. To meet him, you would imagine no other possible provenance than a child's guide for London journalists on how to portray the north. Big and open-faced, frank and very Yorkshire in speech, he always refers to himself just as Rutter, as though Barry were some wimpish affectation. His celebrated theatre company, Northern Broadsides, is cast in the same mould. It lives in a subterranean section of Sir Ernest Hall's mighty palace of culture and business at Dean Clough in Halifax, and its name sounds like the crash of a triple-decker loosing off its guns in Nelson's day. Deliberately so. The company northernises everything it puts on. But then look at its playbill: *Oedipus*, *Antigone* and *The Trackers of Oxyrynchus* by Sophocles, Milton's *Samson Agonistes* and no end of Shakespeare, most recently a production of *Othello* with Lenny Henry in the title role amid a cast of Yorkshire-sounding Venetians at the West Yorkshire Playhouse in Leeds.

Rutter, whose less well-known CV includes a series of cameos at the *Guardian's* mini-pantomime, opera, puppet show and ballet which have entertained successive Christmas parties in the Manchester office, is gregarious and finds no shortage of collaborators in the north. The one who whetted his classical appetite was the poet Tony Harrison, born and educated in Leeds and now living in Newcastle upon Tyne. He has mined his share of old north geology, notably in the poem, *V*, which includes a visit to his parents' grave in a forlorn Leeds cemetery scarred by litter and vandals to an extent worthy of Herbert Whone, the monochromatic chronicler of the 'essential' West Riding (see page 217). But he is also an expert on mediaeval mystery plays and an acclaimed adaptor of Euripides' *Hecuba* and the *Oresteia* of Aeschylus. One of his neighbours in Newcastle is Dr Peter Jones, the constantly bouncy promoter of Friends of Classics, the society 'for all who are interested in and excited by ancient Greece and Rome'. From what he calls 'my Northumbrian fastness,' Jones enthuses schools across the country to restore the study of Latin, Greek and ancient history and astonish a new generation with how much, from democracy to plumbing and steam power, the Classical world understood. He initiates events such as the golden bath sponge competition, in which school students who write mystery stories set in the Graeco-Roman world can win this annual trophy, based on a treasure in a published thriller. I will never forget going to Chester-le-Street to see one of his acolytes, Adrian Spooner, in action at the local Park View comprehensive. Spooner had his Latin and Greek class or Lingo as the school called it – in exuberant, high-voltage form for a full hour. The atmosphere would have delighted the long-dead inhabitants of Conganium, Chester-le-Street in the days of Roman Britain. In a discussion of Graeco-Latin roots of modern words, students came up with tempiphone as an alternative name for the speaking clock. One of the kids asked, mid-discussion: 'Why does dives mean 'rich' when a 'dive' is a dead scruffy place?'

Derek Enright took this northern flair for intellectual fun and vigour to the nation's parliament. After teaching Latin at Hemsworth comprehensive, he became Labour MP for the area and paraded his singing skills, honed at the school, in the chamber of the House of

Commons. 'In natalis oppido,' he struck up in his fine northern baritone, 'erat homo nauticus.' The whole place was soon rocking along to what non-classicists recognised from the tune as Lennon and McCartney's 'Yellow Submarine'.

Do we converse in Latin and Greek in the north then? No, but we do use many more languages and accents than the old north ever did, and to good effect. No one, in my experience, enjoys a monoculture, and the omnipresence of a particular vocabulary or accent can bear heavily on anyone who does not share it, whether the dominance be Geordie, Scouse, Scots or even warm Devonian. It is the dominance which is overbearing, not the accent itself. This was illustrated paradoxically when Leeds' bus-users rose in revolt against an 'extra-received pronunciation' voice which was initially used to make recordings ('This is where to wait for the 28 to Long Causeway …') for the talking bus stops in the central bus station. It smacked too much of overbearing authority in times past, whether from employers, teachers or men and women from the ministry. But there was an irony involved in this. Reporting on the episode, I rang the posh voice's owner, Rowan Morton-Gledhill, then of Radio Leeds, and the poor woman was most upset. 'I come from Huddersfield!' she expostulated. I came away with the impression that the Morton-Gledhills had possibly arrived in the north at the same time as the Viking Hather, whose field probably gave Huddersfield its name. If only she had rounded her vowels and sharpened her As just a tad.

Otherwise, the increasing babel of the north is one of its appeals. I enjoy finding out from bar staff and waitresses which eastern European country they come from. I have grown used to redeploying old skills at detecting a Hull or Wigton accent on the subtle differences in tone, to the English ear, between Czechs and Slovaks. A typical

Liverpool on the brink of regeneration, 1985

example followed a hard day's climb recently round Helvellyn and Catchedicam. The day was topped off by the tearoom in Glenridding, run chaotically but cheerfully by two young Slovenes, who stayed open late for us (and confided their astonishment at the consistency of rock buns, and quite how much cream some people wanted dolloped on their scones).

This is a welcome development from the days when suspicion attended anything so exotic. Charlotte Brontë writes in *Shirley* of how 'an outlandish foreign accent grates on a British and especially a Yorkshire ear.' To underline the point, one of the book's central characters is the innovating mill manager Robert Gerard Moore who is half-Flemish. As relations worsen, he becomes known to his workforce as 'The Devil of Hollows Mill' whereas for his part, he describes the abuse to his friends in much the same terms that a disillusioned West Indian or Pakistani immigrant might have justifiably used in the 1950s: 'I am an alien to these English clowns.'

Today's north shows a brilliant capacity for mocking such prejudice, by turning its surviving purveyors into clowns, literally. Robustly home-grown by talented young students from Bretton Park drama college, near Wakefield, the radio and TV satire *The League of Gentleman* is mercilessly accurate about the insane extremes of 'local-ness' which can still today be encountered in Pennine villages. The nightmarish 'local shop' in the series is a welcome replacement, as fiction, for real-life establishments which were gruesomely similar. Some five years ago, we hosted a young relative of the Irish Nobel laureate Seamus Heaney on work experience in the *Guardian's* Manchester office and he came back from a job in Hadfield – the main model for the league's Royston Vasey – and said: 'There really are people there who always walk to the shops up one side of the street and back down on the other.'

Foreign languages and accents have increased in tandem with far more variants of English than I ever heard as a northern boy. Often, as with the rock buns, they seem to be linked with cuisine. Head south-east from Ullswater and into the Yorkshire Dales, and you find an example of this in the remarkable expertise at making sculptures out of sugar in the Old Hill Inn at Chapel-le-Dale, close to the magnificent Ribblehead railway viaduct on the Settle to Carlisle line (my colleague Denis Thorpe's photograph of a steam engine crossing this mighty structure on a clear day with just a few clouds streaming high up in the sky like an echo of the locomotive's plume of steam is a famous image of the north).

No, making sugar sculpture isn't a traditional northern pastime, but visitors crowd into the modest display which Colin Martin has created in a room behind his otherwise traditional bars. He and his

Colne valley. Tourism joins the mills, 1992

Art in Ian Burke and Susan Sharrard's studio

wife Sabena took over the pub in 2000 after getting tired of London but not of life. Colin made his beautiful set pieces of horse-riders, flowers and animals for military dinners and expensive gambling clubs in the capital, where he was also a sought-after pastry chef. Now he holds classes in both skills up here at the dale head, where the pub has been going since 1608 and guests have included Sir Winston Churchill and countless potholers. Some of the most challenging caves in the country are along the road in Kingsdale and under the Three Peaks of Ingleborough, Penyghent and Whernside. The Old Hill has a wagon wheel as part of its décor and a favourite exercise for cavers is wriggling between the spokes, to check that they are slender or rubbery enough to manage similar squeezes awaiting them underground. The London accents of the Martins (and plenty of their customers) are accepted as happily as Yorkshire and Lancashire ones, and a soft spaniel called Maurice curls up amicably in front of the fire with tough local pointers and setters

Lealholm, base of Eton's art summer schools

brought in by shooting parties.

The presence of a sugar sculpture museum in an out-of-the-way northern village will not surprise modern northerners, for whom heritage has become an important economic staple, a significant way of earning a living. You can imagine the hoo-hah when the prospect of this first became apparent; what a gift to the scornful and the grit-merchants to whom the change from being a miner to dressing up as one in a mining museum was irresistibly symbolic of some sort of emasculation. I remember a classic example in 1987 when a plan was put forward to rebuild Roman Castleford, Legentium, on the 340 acres left derelict by the closure of Glass Houghton pit. Legionnaires and toga-clad citizens were to be recruited from those on the dole, of whom Castleford had many. It was a blackspot which had helped raise unemployment in the Wakefield district to 14 per cent.

Rutter, Tony Harrison and co hadn't quite got steam up by then, which is a shame because they would soon have latched on. Instead, how the cynics mocked. A local councillor told his colleagues during one of many debates: 'No one is waking up at this moment in upstate New York, nudging his missus and saying: "How about going across and taking a look at Castleford?"' A heavyweight book was published in the same month that the plan was unveiled, *The Heritage Industry* by Robert Hewison, which pronounced that what mattered about history like this was that it was over. But it wasn't; it is American tourists who have come over, and heritage and leisure transformations of old industrial sites are symbolic not of castration but of purposeful and profitable change. Legentium was not in the end rebuilt on Glass Houghton, but the enormous and hugely popular Xscape ski slope was, run by the perky French showman Pierre-Yves Gerbeau after his escape from London's great fiasco, the Millennium Dome. Nearby is Diggerland where children (and grown-ups) go wild on JCBs, an adventure which has even been undertaken by an intrigued correspondent from *The Economist*. Assorted restaurants have opened round about, along with shops, and a climbing wall.

Kevin Trickett of Wakefield Civic Society now wants launches from the 13 cruise ships that sail past the Yorkshire coast to come up the river Calder to the city, whose Victorian shipbuilding yards were large and skilled enough to make army freighters which sailed to the Crimea. Meanwhile Bradford succeeded in 2009 in becoming Unesco's first City of Film, using classics such as *Billy Liar* and *Room at the Top* which were filmed locally, as well as the presence of the National Media Museum.

Doncaster pitched in with its Dome, a combination of palm-fronded leisure pool, including a bracing whirlpool section which takes you out of doors, and a beautifully-sculpted skating rink. They craftily trailed this a year earlier, and tested local reaction, by leaking a plan to give the pleasure palace the first nude mixed sauna to be built by an inland local authority. It was a slightly tortuous 'first' but it sat nicely with the overall theme of a campaign called Sunny Donny, which was based on the fact that the town has more sunshine than London on average.

There is nothing demeaning in working in the Dome, or the similar Barnsley Metrodome or the Castleford attractions, any more than the guides at the National Mining Museum feel sissies because they are explaining their subject – knowledgeably and entertainingly – rather than physically hacking away at it. Facework was better paid but I have met only a handful of miners who would have been happy for their sons to follow them down the pit. Part of the kneejerk reaction was an instinctively macho dislike of something that didn't appear to involve sweat. The director of tourism in Hartlepool sussed this in 1980, when he discovered that one way to assuage diehard councillors' suspicions was to talk about his speciality as 'the tourist industry'. When they weren't listening, he added more directly: 'I don't think it really matters if you are throwing molten steel about or throwing cups of tea over customers.'

Heritage work is not remotely the be-all and end-all of the modern northern economy. The mournful, abandoned shipyards on the Wear described in Chapter 1 have been replaced by the equally mammoth Nissan car plant on the hill behind. We will meet many more hi-tech and large-scale arrivals in due course. But it is interesting, involves a range of skills which gets wider as the museum world, IT and educational projects develop, and offers plenty of chances for promotion or moves to other museums, galleries or related projects throughout the country, or indeed the world. Would the north really want to be without Beamish, the Lowry, the Hepworth, Magna, the Sage, the Merseyside museums and indeed Blackpool Pleasure Beach? They are the real result of the 'heritage industry', as opposed to the enjoyable but over-the-top change of roles sentimentally depicted in *The Full Monty*. History is never over. It marches on. The Castleford brigade announced another reconstruction wheeze in February 2009. They want to rebuild Pontefract castle on the site of the Prince of Wales colliery which closed in 2002.

They are also pushing the thought-provoking notion of a National Centre for Intangible Heritage in their town – a place which celebrates local pride and spirit as handed down in stories, songs, dance, photography and film, rather than ancient bricks and mortar like the castle or Castleford's buried Roman walls. They admit that the title sounds like something out of Terry Pratchett's novels, such as the Ministry of Unspellable Spells, but it is all the more intriguing for that. It is purposeful too. Intangible heritage, say the Castleford band, is 'the active engagement of communities with their past, animating them to examine their present needs and create a vision for the future.' Nothing could be less 'over.'

One of the liveliest characters behind these ideas is Brian Lewis, who was a driving force in the Yorkshire Arts Workshop, based in Glasshoughton, which sought out the rich histories hidden in sidelined places and people and turned them into a whole library of short but fascinating books. Lewis deserves a book in himself, but his easy manner disguises occasional but real political influence. Don't forget that the formidable Labour royalty Ed Balls and his wife Yvette Cooper are MPs for the neighbouring constituencies of Pontefract & Castleford and Normanton, so the patch is a good one for exercising clout. Lewis keeps trying to enlist them for another of his heritage enthusiasm: recapturing Robin Hood for Yorkshire from Nottinghamshire.

Throughout my 22 years back in the north, the famous outlaw has been batted to and fro. At the micro-level, the neighbouring

Capturing Robin Hood at Nottingham castle

councils of Kirklees and Calderdale have spatted endlessly over his 'grave', a spurious Victorian construction in the grounds of Kirklees Hall, which is hidden in the trees on the left of the M62 going west just before Junction 25. Every chronicle and legend has Robin dying here, poisoned by the treacherous prioress of Kirklees, but the grave is a folly and the Armytage family, who have sold the hall but own the estate and go back almost as far as the Sheriff of Nottingham, do not encourage anyone to visit it.

Calderdale and Kirklees (which nicked the name to encompass its unhappy marriage of Huddersfield, Dewsbury, Batley and the Holme and Colne valleys) therefore quarrel rather purposelessly over a figure who is almost certainly a creation of popular myth; but the pot of tourist gold which both perceive in the Robin Hood story is real. Nottingham and Nottinghamshire have both prospered on it, which is why the Kirklees quarrel is pursued between them and Yorkshire on a grander scale. Lewis is one of many partisans who deride the lack of evidence linking Robin of Locksley's (Robin Hood) origins and family to Nottingham, other than the troublesome fact that he seems to have spent a lot of time there annoying the sheriff. Lewis has published poems and essays on assorted Yorkshire claimants to the title, while Wakefield council sends details of various 'real' Robin Hoods down the M1 regularly, once in the care of a Maid Marian in medieval costume astride a 750cc motorbike. Doncaster's new airport on the huge former RAF Finningley base has meanwhile been called Robin Hood. And the former Labour MP for Wakefield David Hinchliffe has tried repeatedly to get the government, the Highways Agency or anyone really, to remove Nottingham's border road signs which boldly welcome drivers to Robin Hood Country. The media treat the whole thing as fun, understandably, but the participants are serious people (Hinchliffe has a huge northern following from the time he was parliament's voice of rugby league), and serious money is involved. When Nottingham city council commissioned a firm of London brand specialists to discover what outsiders knew about the place, the answer came back in précis: Robin Hood and not much else.

Look how other northern cities have benefited. Ever since 2003, Manchester has been the third most popular city or town in Britain for visitors from overseas (after London and Edinburgh) and Liverpool jumped 10 places in 2005 to rank sixth, a position it has held since then, fortified by its successful year in 2008 as European Capital of Culture. England's north country (the Visit Britain definition of the three northern regions plus the Isle of Man) attracted 2,480,000 visitors in 2000 who spent an estimated £870 million. By 2008, the numbers had risen to 4,020,000 spending £1,504 million. In all three regions, tourism is in the top 10 business sectors and all are naturally bidding for a share of the practice camps, events and extra visitors which are expected to come with the 2012 London Olympics. Manchester showed its mettle in that regard with the successful staging of the 2002 Commonwealth games when even the tipping rain during the closing ceremony didn't damp the feeling of élan at a job well done. A week of Royal Ascot in York in 2004, when the official course in Berkshire was being restored and improved, brought an extra 250,000 visitors to the city.

Tourism is not a cure-all and shares the vulnerability of any industry to recession or changing public taste; the Robin Hood Experience in Nottingham grew increasingly tatty and has recently fallen on hard times. But it has the intrinsic virtue that a place which people want to visit is usually a place where others like to live. When the Government relocated the headquarters of the National Health Service to Leeds in 1992, staff had to be issued with reassuring survival kits, which was good news for the former *Sunday Times* journalist Roger Ratcliffe. He had himself relocated and not only survived but has written an upbeat book called *Leeds Fax*. The government bought 2,500 copies. This was not considered necessary for any of the agencies which have moved to tourist-rich York from the south east over the years, such as the Central Science Laboratory and the National Curriculum Council. The more modest beauties of Howden, coupled to eight direct services a day to the capital run by the excellent Hull Trains, attracted the Press Association to shift so much of its London operation to East Yorkshire that every other person you meet in the town is an IT technician or a subeditor. They are not paid over-handsomely, but lower prices for everything from houses to groceries is another benefit of moving to their new home from London.

Halifax's future reflects the past

Awareness of the value of beautiful landscape or past heritage even enhances the activities of heavy industry which in the past did so much to damage both. Beside the M62 near Selby, a triangular micro-world connects the Kellingley colliery – Big K, whose 600 staff hold European records for production – with Eggborough power station and the Gale Common ash disposal site. Big K and Eggborough are not things of beauty, but Gale Common is, deliberately. Its artificial hill, which is essentially a slagheap, is modest in height compared to the northern fells but it towers over the flat local landscape. For this reason, the then National Coal Board employed the distinguished landscape architect Brenda Colvin to design it, which she did on the lines of an ancient hillfort, with thoughtful planting which has made the area a haven for wildlife and interesting plants. In the lea of Gale Common, the supermarket Asda is trialling the growing of truffles as a potential upmarket line for its stores. The idyllic picture will be complete when someone restores the former gourmet reputation of the Ancient Shepherd pub in the nearby hamlet, Cridling Stubbs.

Heritage interest has reinforced the appeal of urban development too, particularly in waterside flats and the conversion of former industrial buildings. The modern skyline of Manchester has its roots not only in a demand for something new, but also in the fondness for the city's past which was shared by a group of unofficial movers and shakers in the mid-1990s. Tony Wilson of Factory Records, the Hacienda club and Granada TV was one of them. So was the architect Alan Simpson, Tom Bloxham of the developers Urban Splash and his co-director Nick Johnson who started the Atlas bar and was primarily responsible for bringing back inner-city living in Manchester for the young and aspiring.

They were among the audience when Marketing Manchester breathlessly unveiled a stunningly banal advertising campaign with the slogan: 'Manchester's up and going.' Their common reaction – 'you cannot be serious!' – led to the formation of a discussion group which they called the McEnroe Club. This had no official status but was influential, with city officials including the council's chief executive Sir Howard Bernstein attending its get-togethers to talk about Manchester's future. It was soon followed by a similar exercise in Leeds which was going to be called the FU Club, linking the might-have-been Quarry Hill flats naval signal flags to the curious fact that all planning applications in Leeds have a code which ends FU. The group chickened out in the end, because cheeking the planners was not part of the plan. Both clubs were co-operative and friendly initiatives, concentrating on getting things done.

They were never highly organised and have waxed and waned in the 12 years since the McEnroe was formed, but there have been significant moments of renewed enthusiasm. In 2000, Bloxham and co launched an equally informal action group called the Manchester Independents. The aim was to make the city as friendly as possible to independent businesses rather than multiples and multinationals, which were not rejected but would come anyway. The essential point was made by Bloxham: 'Independents generate wealth that stays here. Our money doesn't go off to the City. It's spent in the local economy.'

There is an appealing lightheartedness to all this. Urban Splash has a humorous way with its projects: its splendid revival of Manningham Mills in Bradford included wooden baths, which led to much scepticism about splinters in the bottoms of loft-purchasers. In Salford's previously unfashionable Langworthy district, the developers created an area called Chimney Pot Park where rows of traditional terraces were turned on their heads: living rooms are upstairs and bedrooms down on the ground floor.

The Press Association in Howden

This is new but it also has roots in the past. Northerners forgot too much, during the years of decline, how much zip there had been in previous days. Recall what delicate energy shines through the drawings of Phil May or what fun they had in Manchester and Liverpool's theatreland in the 19th century's naughty nineties. Why get solemn about the heritage industry when a little village called Crofton near Wakefield pluckily joins in, helped admittedly by Andy Green, a canny PR man who lives there, and launches a tourist initiative on the back of its Leaning Fish & Chip Shop? As tilted as the Tower of Pisa, they said, subtly linking one northern speciality – fish and chips – to another – coal-mining subsidence. The chip shop's attractions were also backed by an attractively self-deprecating list of moments in history when Crofton narrowly missed fame: Sir Titus Salt would have built his famous alpaca mills there had not neighbouring landlords objected and forced him to go to Saltaire, near Bradford, which is now one of Britain's 24 World Heritage Sites as a result. John Harrison, inventor of the chronometer and solver of the longitude puzzle, may have lived there, but neighbouring Nostell also claims him and neither can prove it; finally, Elizabeth Brontë, the older sister of the famous literary trio, went to school in Crofton and, had she lived might have written an even greater novel than *Jane Eyre* or *Wuthering Heights* and thereby put the place on the tourist trail. This was micro-tourism, but indicative of an enthusiasm which has spread far beyond the major visitor attractions. On the Brontë front, another fine example of mini-heritage, all the better for poking fun with a light touch, was the pub at Haworth which created a room in honour of the unknown (because entirely fictional) Brontë brothers and sisters. They had carried out balloon ascents, climbed unconquered mountains, that sort of thing. This was derivative,

Tony Wilson, the Manchester Man

although none the less entertaining for that. The joke had previously been made by Michael Wharton, the renegade Bradfordian at the *Daily Telegraph* between 1957 and 2006 whose *Way of the World* column written as Peter Simple included a character called Doreen Brontë, who allegedly used to dress up as her brother Branwell to drink in Haworth's pubs and founded the village girls' small bore rifle club.

Another *Way of the World* institution was Alderman Foodbotham, the '25-stone, crag-visaged, iron watch-trained perpetual chairman of Bradford Tramways and Fine Art Committee.' Such hallucinatory creations were the work of a man who knew that the real Bradford was very different. He was the son of a German-Jewish businessman in Bradford called Nathan (Wharton was his mother's name) and he was brought up in a cultured, cosmopolitan community which another illustrious son of the city, JB Priestley, described as resembling 'a dash of the Rhine and the Oder' in the mucky Bradford Beck. That too is the world returning in the north, even if the media describe such things as 'multicultural', reserving the more appealing adjective 'cosmopolitan' for London and the south.

I will return to the north's cosmopolis in Chapter 7, but in terms of a wider variety of native British comers-in, we have never been better served than we are today, thanks particularly to the region's universities. As you get older, to walk along Oxford road in Manchester, round Hope Street in Liverpool or in Jesmond, Newcastle, increasingly feels like passing a succession of primary schools at break. Young people swarm everywhere, and they come from all over the country. They enjoy their time in the north, to the extent that in 1999 urban geographers financed by the Economic and Social Research Council described the Headingley area of Leeds as 'a Shangri-La for students.' Further, argued the report's author Dr David Clarke, who worked as a geographer at Leeds University within quarter of a mile of his survey patch and was thus well-placed to judge, the grids of stone and redbrick terraces were 'perfection for twenty and thirty-somethings,' a bonus in terms of retaining students after graduation. They like it so much that, if practicable, they stay.

You get a sense of this if you take the two-car Northern Rail train from Leeds to York (advertised on the station noticeboards, be warned, as from Burley Park to Poppleton because the quicker route between the two cities is the direct one through Garforth, and they don't want passengers who are in a hurry complaining). The diesel trundles right past backyards where in summer students revise in the sun. At Burley Park and Headingley halts, they hop on or off with their teetering piles of books and lecture notes, music buzzing from their headphones. I followed Dr Clarke's theories up on the ground and found nothing to contradict them. Pottering out to buy milk from the Granbys, a box of brick terraces just behind Headingley's main shops, 21-year-old Craig Hornsby told me: 'I'm definitely more bothered about living round here than I am about getting myself a career at this stage. You've got everything from takeaways and friends to the whole Leeds Rhinos team in the Skyrack pub on Sunday night.' Reminiscing about barbecues that turned seamlessly into parties involving the whole street, he planned to buy a house locally after getting his maths degree at Leeds University. Bhairvee Malik, a 20-year-old house-hunting in the Granbys for her second year of reading English and history, agreed: 'I call Headingley 'pyjama town', because you can go out in the street in your pyjamas and no one bats an eyelid.' Those who persist in believing in grimness and rain will be incredulous that one of Leeds' major planning issues in the Spring of 2009 revolved round a plan to build permanent barbecue sites for Shangri-La citizens on nearby Woodhouse Moor.

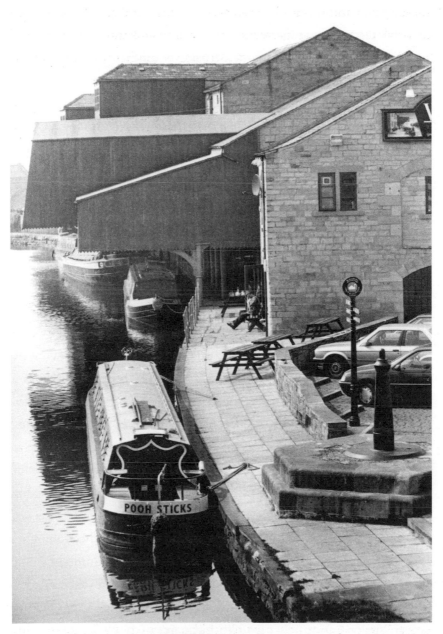

The cut at Blackburn, restored with EU funds

A successful example of staying put is Joanne Harris, the writer of *Chocolat* and a series of other inventive novels, who spent her childhood in her grandparents' sweet shop in Barnsley and still lives nearby. There's something about Barnsley sweetshops; the actor Brian Glover was born in one run by his parents. Harris's father Bob grew up among the jars of Yorkshire Mixture and chocolate bars, before travelling in France and meeting Joanne's French mother Jeanette at a dance in Brittany. He brought her back to Barnsley, where they both taught French and filled their house with books. Joanne went to Cambridge University but she too returned north, bringing her husband Kevin back and playing bass and flute in a local rock band, while teaching French herself and working in spare time on the novels. Kevin did drums and vocals in the same combo.

Just up the road from them lives another northerner, Rita Britton, whose Pollyanna fashion business has never left Barnsley but is known across the world. She has succeeded on talent and energy, plus luck that her youthful energy and boldness coincided with the 1960s when similar entrepreneurs such as John Stephen, the Glasgow welder's apprentice who made Carnaby Street's name, saw what the big stores were not doing, and did it. Youth was at the helm and little capital was needed, luckily because Britton was brought up in a two-up, two-down with a tin bath, moved to a Sheffield council estate and failed her eleven-plus. She didn't mind. She saw beyond all that. Fed up with a drudge job at a paper mill, whose days she anyway reckoned were numbered, she rang up the fashion designer Ossie Clark from a phone box at the end of her grandmother's road and blagged him into promising to buy from her if she succeeded in her dream of setting up her own design business. Her father, a lorry driver, scraped together a loan to back her own £500 savings and she opened a shop, in a damp Barnsley basement with blacked-out

Ferrybridge. One of the Dreadnoughts on the M62

windows, but with an order from Clark. Forty years later, Polyanna's shop and café in a four-storey, Georgian house on Market Hill is listed by the Victoria and Albert Museum among the leading shops of the world.

Britton illustrates the fact that modernising northerners need not be an outside implant – although many have been – but a native development. Her work, like Harris's, acknowledges the north's abiding virtues and builds on them, and sometimes makes use of its vices as well. Polyanna's surge to success and fame was significantly helped when a fashion-writer from the *Daily Telegraph*, Hilary Alexander, who was less London-bound or Milan-fixated than some, heard about this then-curious Yorkshire outpost and came to have a look. Britton, typically, was not nonplussed by a national newspaper showing interest, and when she met Alexander at the station, she warned her: 'If this article is going to be a mickey-take of Barnsley, let's forget the whole thing.' Alexander was sensible and perceptive. She didn't plan to take the mick, but she told Britton: 'Don't forget, you are receiving this publicity partly because of where you are.' Britton didn't, and her thorough way of doing things in Barnsley acknowledges, as Harris has done in lyrical passages about the town in her novels, that its old north image has played a part in her success.

It was Barnsley again which won enormous publicity for the architect Will Alsop's theoretical redesign of its centre in 2003 as an Italian hill village with an encircling 'wall' of curious new buildings. There was a modicum of chortling and some wry comments from those unreconstructed Old northerners from the town, exile Sir Michael Parkinson and loyal native Dicky Bird; but the scheme, and more importantly the innovative, questioning frame of mind which it hoped to encourage among local people, got enormous publicity. Barnsley was a bit cynical, especially when Alsop added with a flourish the idea of a halo cast by searchlights into the sky above the town hall. But it also felt, a little smugly: that's right. The world is sitting up and taking notice of us. These benefits came from a masterplan which has so far remained more of an idea than a reality, but that adds to its interest. Other 'starchitects' have contributed iconic buildings to the north in the last 20 years, such as Daniel Liebeskind's Imperial War Museum North on the Trafford bank of Salford Quays, or Lord Foster's glazed armadillo at The Sage in Gateshead. But Barnsley shows how much transformation can follow simply from refreshing ideas.

All sorts of things about the town were unearthed by curious national journalists following up the Alsop story. Instead of the usual, unoriginal references to Parkinson, coal-mining and the giant Barnsley lamb chop, we were told how most of Britain's milk bottles were made in the town, and the tennis balls used in Wimbledon championships. The councillors responsible for commissioning Alsop, under an excellent programme of the regional development agency Yorkshire Forward, called Renaissance Towns, were also praised officially for showing the sort of can-do attitude and willingness to change which South Yorkshire needed after the collapse of coal.

Visiting the town in 2004, the Audit Commission went out of its way to commend the depth of support for Steve Houghton, the council's Labour leader, who promoted the Alsop project and allied novel ideas in the face of many entrenched attitudes. The report of the commission's regeneration inspection said that Houghton had achieved 'a critical break with the past' and carried with him not only his Cabinet and senior officers, but members of other parties – a breakaway group of Labour independents which was jostling for power, Liberals and Tories. *The Municipal Journal* added a helpful national perspective to what might otherwise have subsided gradually into a purely local success. In 2007 Houghton was voted one of the two best council leaders in the country in a poll of readers.

Was it depressing, then, to attend the local council election count in May 2008 and find Houghton scraping back in with a majority of one? No, because another essential part of the north today is the destruction of monolithic centres of single party power. It is not the political colours of the process that matter, but the fact that local decision-makers are more diverse and, above all, that they have simply changed. The Labour party in places such as Sheffield, Liverpool and Newcastle upon Tyne became arthritic and wrapped in golden memories of its often genuinely glorious past. In Bradford and Doncaster, it rotted and turned corrupt. We have not entered a glorious new dawn as a result, but the fact that a man as capable as Houghton has to fight tooth and nail for his reforms is entirely welcome. True, there could be battles royal within the old, monolithic party states, among the many factions out of which a simple-sounding entity such as 'Labour' was formed. But as far as most of us in the north were concerned, they took place in the dark.

Apart from northerners in the north there are other lively modernisers, thinkers and critics in a diaspora which extends as far as the more famous dispersals of the Irish, Jews and Sri Lankan Tamils. One of the most enjoyable parts of my work is compiling a weekly email called *The Northerner*, which selects the interesting, unusual and entertaining from the northern media and supplies it in a précis with added comments and reflections, prompted by both the stories and the wider northern experiences of myself and my alternate writers, Helen Carter and Mark Smith. Email responses show how many of its readers are scattered all over the world; to mention a Malton pie or a walk to the pepperpot Hoad monument above Ulverston (a memorial to Sir John Barrow, a founder member of the Royal Geographical Society), is to prompt a nostalgic message from Buenos Aires, Florida or points just about anywhere else. Likewise, the online version of a newspaper such as the *Oldham Chronicle* has an expats' section which you can activate by clicking on any of a sprinkling of coloured pins, all over the world. If you do, up come little biographies and messages, for instance when I last looked there was Mark Heap sending regards from Shanghai and Don Munro managing an export company in Hangzhou where he 'works hard, plays hard and welcomes visitors.' Not far away was Michael Boardman whose choice of career was no doubt influenced by the extraordinary number of holes dug through the Pennines, to take railways and canals between Yorkshire and Lancashire. He said 'Hi to everyone in Oldham!' from Shanghai, where he was building railway tunnels. The *Huddersfield Examiner* plays a different game with technology, soliciting exiles to send in photographs of distant places in which the spirit of the town has been planted. Thus we get

X-ray diffraction specialists at Daresbury

Carl Bleduklewicz posing in the snow beside a company helicopter which zooms him round Australia selling furniture. Or Neil Pilling comparing Ho Chi Minh city where he teaches to his previous life as assistant manager of Huddersfield town hall.

I have had plenty of these exiles among my own colleagues, and the refreshing characteristic of almost all of them, as with the Oldham and Huddersfield expats, is that they are missionaries for the north rather than fugitives from it. I remember in particular a leisurely conversation with my colleague Gary Finn, a night news editor, because it involved one of the most extraordinary northern images in all my experience. I knew Gary a little in his previous job at the *Yorkshire Post* and we got chatting about his local origins.

His father worked as a maintenance engineer on the huge cooling towers of Ferrybridge power station, a sister-plant to Eggborough which marks the junction of the great north road and the transpennine

M62. Part of his work involved slinging a container inside the towers to use like a window-cleaners' platform for checking the structure. These towers' predecessors, you may remember, were involved in an extraordinary exposure of unforeseen and, to be fair, unlikely design flaws when their shape and positioning funnelled 85mph winds inside each of the eight towers that whirled round, each in a vortex, causing vibrations which shattered three of the towers and left the other five irreparably damaged. Finn senior and his colleagues had a role in checking that the reinforced replacements held firm.

His mother was meanwhile working in a layby café just down the road, where normally she could take young Gary. But one day, she fell sick and the family's various alternative arrangements for babysitting also fell through. Thus it was that Gary was looked after, high above the chasm of one of the Ferrybridge towers, in his father's platform, which resembled an aerial fishing boat. 'It must have been awesome,' I marvelled, imagining the small child slung amid the steam which

Suite view from Liverpool's Hope Street boutique hotel

rises from the power stations along the M62 like the funnel smoke columns of a Great War dreadnought fleet. 'It must have been,' he agreed. 'But I was asleep.'

Finn's insouciance is symbolic of the way that exiles from the north keep its flag flying: not in the nostalgic-for-trams-'n'-cobbles style of the previous generation, but with a recognition of how the regions have changed and what they are like now. Like the trams themselves, communications have improved so much that a day return to the north is no longer an eccentricity, even if it is expensive. An indicator of the change has been the gradual withdrawal of railway sleeping cars; when I started on the *London Evening Standard* in 1975, I could still take this stately method of travel with my own bed, with heating-steam hissing from various points beneath the carriage, a bottle of water and in the morning, tea and a biscuit from the attendant who, to complete the joy, was usually a cheerful, plump man called Mr Wainwright.

Not any more. As I write in the spring of 2009, the associated luxury of eating a proper meal on the trains north is facing the buffers. National Express has cut the number of breakfast, lunch and tea services it inherited from the former franchisee, Great North-eastern Railways, from 96 to 15 and made ominous noises about the whole idea of silver service and a choice of wines on wheels being at odds with the recession. Virgin's Pendolinos likewise limit dinner to first class and do not offer it at all on their super voyager services between Birmingham and Scotland. It is hard to argue the point financially, although if I had the Desert Island Discs' choice of one luxury, it would be a Euston-Manchester or King's Cross-Leeds diner. But trains are now almost too fast for anyone to enjoy a proper meal on the journey. North and south are so close that passengers risk indigestion.

Don your tekkie anoraks, too, because the internet is the other redoubtable bond between absent northerners and the reality of change in the world they have left behind. If an exiled Leeds woman forgets the effect on her home city of Harvey Nichols – and haven't I been restrained in not mentioning that mighty changer of the north's image until page 82 – she has endless Facebook, Twitter, Flickr and Skype opportunities to check that the shop is still there. Online bonding completes the ties that hold together those who have gone and those who remain. A particularly enjoyable way of appreciating this, is to join the mighty battle between two rival Facebook pages which in 2010 will celebrate its fourth year.

One is called '1,000 Reasons why the north is better than the south', and the other, unthinkably, '1,000 reasons why the south is better than the north'. It began when a 21-year-old student from Haltwhistle in Northumberland, Gary Allison, set up the pro-north

New trade: wine leaves Liverpool for Manchester by barge

page and within days was posting a message on it marvelling: 'This is bigger than we thought.' Thousands of people messaged him with their reasons, ranging from basics such as 'better sheep' to the surreal: 'policeman from space' and 'inability to die.' Under the system of 'Friends' which Facebook encourages for its pages, Allison had over 70,000 when the project celebrated its first birthday in 2007.

His original modest aim was just to wind up his best friend, a bold explorer from the London suburb of Orpington called Phil Anderton who had come up to Tyneside to study at university in Newcastle. It was Anderton who hit back with the rival page, which in recent times has been invaded by northern correspondents, resulting in a welter of the internet's trademark abuse. Only a researcher of enormous persistence would take up Facebook's cheery suggestion of clicking on a hyperlink 'to see all 30,862 posts' (the south) or 48,386 ones (the north), but that ratio has marked the battle for at least two years. In early 2008, *The Journal* in Newcastle picked up the story and reported that the north had around 102,000 friends while the south trailed with about 80,000. When I looked in March 2009, the north had pulled away to 116,897, leaving the south at 89,480.

This hi-tech world is part of a growing base of science in the north – for example, at Daresbury in Cheshire (the Science and Technology Facilities' laboratories) and Sand Hutton near York (the Central Science Laboratory for the Department for Environment, Food and Rural Affairs). Newcastle upon Tyne has an exceptional concentration of stem cell skill (the Institute of Human Genetics) and marine biology (the Dove Marine Laboratory which is at the centre of the largest university marine department in Britain). Salford University is the country's leader in 'virtual world' technology and the Cumbrian coast, for better or worse, is becoming Britain's biggest and most concentrated centre of skills and technology involved in civil nuclear power. Britain's nuclear reprocessing and decommissioning industry is based there and as part of the government's 'nuclear renaissance', three new power stations are planned to join the complex at Sellafield, where the Calder Hall plant was the world's first nuclear power station when it opened in 1956. The heritage people have their eye on that too; Clifford Jones of Lancaster University, nicknamed the 'nuclear archaeologist', wants to make an historic and tourist attraction of the buildings, which stopped generating power in 2003. It could revive the fortunes of the Sellafield visitor centre, which at its peak in the 1990s drew on the Lake District's mass of visitors to attract 1,000 visitors a day. Selby has meanwhile led Britain's bid for the European Spalliation Source, a neutron accelerator and collider, and Hull University is the first port of call for specialist enquiries about coastal erosion. Slingsby Aviation makes military training aircraft on the edge of the North York Moors national park at Kirbymoorside and Systagenix Wound Management produces highly specialised dressings and plasters at Gargrave just outside the Yorkshire Dales national park.

The last two reinforce the argument about the spin-offs from tourism and its care of the landscape. As well as being sited in beautiful places where people enjoy living, they also provide a welcome range of jobs from management to part-time cleaning, in areas where since 2000 the traditional staple of farming has employed fewer people than the voluntary sector. And they are not cut off; indeed in future they have every prospect of becoming closer to the heart of the European Union than if they were down south. How so? The answer involves a party trick which Paul Jagger, chair of the Trade Union Congress in Yorkshire and the Humber, and I have played regularly during annual visits by students on the leadership courses run by the Royal College of Defence Studies. These groups are made up of bright young military officers from all over the world, whose governments want to enlarge their knowledge of political affairs. To the college's credit, the programme always includes a regional tour, as well as a thorough introduction to the heart of British government in London.

Our trick was to take the standard map of Britain and Europe, with the country 'sitting' vertically above France and what seems to be the obvious Dover/Calais crossing to the continent, and turn it 90 degrees clockwise. Suddenly the best option is not so obvious after all. Instead, the Humber estuary, Britain's busiest group of ports and swiftly reachable from the north, midlands or Scotland without enduring the congestion of the south east, now looks like the gateway to the low countries, and to Germany, the Baltic and Russia. Just as Liverpool prospered in the heyday of transatlantic shipping to the new world, so the North Sea ports are beginning to do the same with the new Europe; and Liverpool and Manchester are not left out. They are linked to the Humber by the M62, M18 and M180 – and on that score, what we need to do now is to follow the example of Ireland and put up new motorway signs. Every blue one saying M62 should have a green counterpart, reminding drivers that it is also European route E20, which links some of the continent's busiest manufacturing centres between St Petersburg and Shannon. Or as some of us in the north are starting to call it: the outer London bypass.

3

Combining the Values

'That bright household in our joyous north.'
Algernon Charles Swinburne
'Sonnet to William Bell Scott' 1882

I came back to the north with my family on September 2 1987 after working away for nearly twenty years. Penny, my wife, had made regular trips up the M1 with me but for our two small boys it was almost all new. They careered off into our new and improbably large garden and set about assimilating at the same time, in the school and playgroup just up the hill.

That was our first change and challenge, when we turned up with the other parents at collecting time. When the children spilled out of our primary school in Chiswick, they were every colour imaginable, hair and skin; here in Leeds, there initially seemed to be 30-something small Wainwrights, all of them pink cheeked and fair-haired. For the young 'incomers' themselves, adjustment was a matter of speech and accent, not appearance. We knew that all was well when, only a few weeks into their new world, the boys raced home to announce that the PTA was laying on a film in the assembly hall, the Disney classic about Herbie the Volkswagen. 'Moom, moom!' they shouted with the long 'U's which mark Yorkshire people's speech, 'It's the Loove Boog."

It was the small differences everyone noticed first; and since the first thing you do in new surroundings is say 'Hello' to your neighbours, the very first was in speech. This is a rich and fascinating subject in any part of the country; I still enjoy mimicking the Ls which Bristolians add to any word ending in A; and when it comes to discussing the north's famous use of the word 'love', I cede precedence to the way I was often addressed in Bath by older men as 'My lover.'

But there has been no fall-off in the use of 'love' as a term of greeting during my 22 years back here; indeed, I only recently came across a nice misunderstanding of the word's different usages in the

Yorkshire Street in Lancashire Rochdale, 1972

caption of a framed photograph given by university colleagues to a friend. The text which they sent to the (Yorkshire) framer read: To Colin, love from your university mates. When he unwrapped the gift, the engraved words read: To Colin love, from your university mates.

The spirited survival of northern speech – indeed, its recovery and advance during my lifetime, with the easing of social stuffiness and the benign effect of TV's babel of voices – is a real virtue of life here, and an attraction. Geordie, Scouse, Yorkshire, Lancashire and Cumbrian have not simply survived the attempt to impose received pronunciation (RP) which began with the Victorians and persisted until after the second world war. You no longer need to speak proper if you want to get on. Local voices have turned the tables on that, as well as the now-defunct but once powerful belief that, just as we would all have infinite leisure time and zoom around in space pods thanks to robots, so we would speak a universal 'BBC English'. Today's BBC is chirrupy with the likes of Ant and Dec, and Big Brother is only the best-known of many programmes whose commentary comes in the accents and speech patterns of the north. The failure of RP discipline, with its flutterings at a dropped H, is symbolised for ever by northerners' joyous addition of an H everywhere that it isn't supposed to be. My favourite is the HaichSBC bank. This isn't exclusively northern; until recently London had the example of Arding & Hobbs department store in Lavender Hill which put most newcomers' tongues in a twist. But it is particularly strong here. Northern English must have contributed to that famous linguistic mixture, Maltese, which has an extra letter H in its alphabet, with two crossbars to show you to Haich it.

In terms of accent, life is more interesting and socially united this way, and local speech has roots which were only damaged, not dug up, by the 19th century's crusade to impose on everyone the grammar and accents which had previously marked out the powerful and well-to-do. At primary school, the children had a tape about the Armada which featured discussions between Sir Francis Drake, Lord Howard and Sir John Frobisher. They spoke respectively with a rich Devon voice, a 'proper' RP one and a west Yorkshire accent, which is almost certainly how things were in 1588. All were important people but they were from different parts of the country, rather than all based in London. It was good to experience the benign effect of this on a generation so many years later. 'One of the admirals came from round here,' the children explained to us over tea. Strictly speaking, Frobisher was from Wakefield rather than north Leeds, but it is close enough.

The survival of northern grammar is even more interesting than accent, and perhaps has additional virtue because it is less bedevilled by snobbery. Over the years I have compiled an enormous dictionary of word differences between Yorkshire and London – things 'go off' in the north rather than 'go on'; you don't 'pop' out for forgotten shopping, you 'bob'. And of course there is the specially rich vocabulary of love. But the real masterclass comes with structural differences such as 'It's a cool place, is Manchester' or 'That chair wants mending.' My heart lifts when I hear one of these, doubly so if it comes in the otherwise unrevealing speech of a northerner whose accent has gone or who never had one in the first place. Why? Because they anchor both speaker and spoken-to to familiar and common ground. The more delicately nuanced they are, the greater the pleasure, as happens when an entire episode of your life is recalled, however briefly, by a particular smell. Morrison Supermarkets emphasise their northern origins through their practice of putting signs at the exits of all their car parks saying 'See You Later' – like the added H, not an exclusively northern usage but unusual here in that almost everyone says it, causing in my experience confusion among London visitors. They give that brief look of alarm that some appointment has skipped their minds, because they don't know that it simply means 'Goodbye.'

It may be that with its recent expansion, Morrisons has become just another vast supermarket firm but, for my generation, its northernness will take a long time to die. Until the company took over Safeway, carrying a Morrisons' bag in London was a signal to other northerners in the capital: 'I'm one too.' Now we have to use Booths' bags instead. I'm also proud to have won the *Yorkshire Post* business question of the year award in 2004 for asking Sir Ken Morrison for a guarantee that they would continue selling bilberries – the only big supermarket chain to do so. The bottles of lusciousness come from Poland, admittedly, but the bilberry would run away with the title if we were ever to copy the states of the US and have an official northern fruit.

Another linguistic trap for outsiders is the baby haddock, one of several pitfalls for those unused to the etiquette of the northern fish and chip shop. We open our mouths first to speak, then we use them to eat; and northern food has been a matter for wonderment and very large plates since time began. The baby haddock is not a slimmers' option but an extra-large portion, just as the scallop in a fish and chip shop has nothing to do with dainty bites of shellfish. It is a very big chip coated in batter. Famously, the Conservative cabinet minister Sir Keith Joseph exclaimed in a chippie in Brighouse during the 1983 election campaign: 'Just look! Scallops only cost 20p here' and started to use this apparent bargain to promote Margaret Thatcher's handling of the economy. Actually, in 1983 20p was quite a lot to pay for our northern sort of scallop, although you got plenty of wholesome carbohydrates for your money.

Fish and chips is one of the region's cardinal virtues, so therefore an object of exceptional and sustained loyalty. The meal is still the most popular takeaway in Britain after all these years of tasty pizzas and lovely, ingenious curry. Its past contains some of the most trenchant statements of northernness in our whole history of trumpeting and boasting. A poll taken early in 2009 shows why this is justified: 60 per cent of southerners agreed that northern chips were better, and 93 per cent of northerners. I have a classic account by the Friendly Band, from the corduroy-making village of Friendly in Calderdale, who went to play in London in 2005. Their newsletter's report, after referring to 'typical London drivers who blocked one junction after another', delaying their coach, concludes with the band secretary's description of a disastrous lunch (or dinner as most northerners would call it): 'It is not advisable to sample the "traditional British Fish & Chips" on offer at £5.95 per serving, until the shop has been visited by the local environmental health department.'

Such disdain turns to furious emotion, however, when the debate moves into the north itself and partisans of the different sub-regions get going. Here's an example of how passion for a simple food can run high: Lancashire fries fish and chips in oil, overwhelmingly; Yorkshire uses beef dripping (which tastes particularly good at the Yorkshire Fisheries chip shop in Ramsbottom, an outpost of best practice in Lancashire). In 1917 the Lancashire friers tried to extend their oily empire by supporting the wartime government's concern about a shortage of stearine, which is used in making munitions and comes from animal fat. Look at all this dripping being used in Yorkshire they said, taking advantage of their dominant position in the National Federation of Fish Friers at the time. The reaction from the other side of the Pennines was thunderous. Yorkshire chip shops broke away and formed the Northern Counties Federation of Fish Friers and their magazine *The Frier* explained why: 'Animal fat is

Sir Ken Morrison; a man who knows his job

the food of a dominant people. The cry for vegetable oil throughout the country was for the feeding of an inferior people. Animal fat for the dominant race. Animal fat for the dominant county within that race.'

I told this story, which is described at length in John Walton's masterly *Fish and Chips and the British Working Class 1870-1940*, a couple of years ago to Headingley Townswomen's Guild and a woman, her face shining, came up afterwards and gave me even stronger proof of the faith that dripping attracts. I had not believed that *The Frier's* editorial could be bettered, but it was. 'We had an air raid shelter made from dripping, during the war,' she said. 'Tell me more,' I said in amazement, and she did. Her father ran a chip shop in Birstall and mistrusted the hard edges of the corrugated iron Anderson and Morrison shelters on offer from the Home Office. His dripping came in blocks like bricks which he stored in the keeping cellar. 'He put two and two together, and before long we had a cellar lined with dripping, floor to ceiling, which is where we went when the sirens sounded,' she said. 'It would have been squashy, I suppose, like an airbag in a car.' I didn't like to ask if her father had thought about incendiary bombs, knowing what he must have done about things frying.

There is another peculiarity which the northern fish and chip shop contributes to our sense of community, and of the different, independent-minded habits, which is this chapter's theme. It is the fact that its opening times are a science in themselves and, like Ken Morrison's 'See you later' have the additional attraction of catching outsiders out. I still get a warm feeling when I remember reporting an election in the 1980s and watching a party of Young Conservatives from southern constituencies beaver conscientiously away, pushing leaflets through doors in the Pennine town of Honley, until it was time for their dinner at 1pm. Oh dear. That is when northern fish and chip shops (outside such highly sophisticated places as Manchester or Leeds) shut.

I like buying my own fish and chips in Yeadon, from an inconspicuous chippie at the bottom of the Steep which appears in the local phone book as 'Oldest Fish and Chip Shop in the World, The': it was founded in the 1870s. That's pretty impressive, although Lees of Mossley in Greater Manchester claims to have been founded in 1863 and, disconcertingly for northerners, the national federation decided in 1968, after three years of research, that Malin's of Bow, founded either in 1860 or in 1865, was the first fish and chip shop. But neither Malin's nor Lees has ever had a frier who appeared on a TV documentary about naturists, showing (in every sense) how the Yeadon frier and and his wife spent their spare time when well away from hot dripping. Customers looked at him thoughtfully after the programme was shown. But then, they may just have been trying to work out the opening times, which even by northern chip shop standards were byzantine.

Oldest Fish and Chip Shop in the World, The, opened and closed almost like the badgers on the TV comedy *The Fast Show* which appeared when nature enthusiast Bob Fleming looked away or had yet another coughing fit, and vanished as soon as he turned round again. Days were different, lunch/dinners and tea/suppers came at surprisingly varied times and it was all an excellent challenge and, crucially, not the same as the timings anywhere else. Local, distinctive, good. And a way to earn a living that is taken very seriously. At the Thomas Danby catering college in Leeds, the national federation, which is based in the city, sponsors courses to refresh members' skills as well as introductory sessions for the surprisingly large number of people from all sorts of previous backgrounds who fancy opening a chip shop. I went to the first morning of a four-day course run by Brian Morton, who swapped turbine management at a power station in Capetown for running a chippie on an estate in Leeds.

'There's tower blocks, a pub, an elderly people's home next door and a working men's club beyond that,' he told us. 'It's a magical spot for selling fish and chips.' Then he switched off the lights and showed us a film called *A Day in the Life of a Fish Frier*, starring a woman who could get 85 portions out of one stone of fish. 'You beginners'll be lucky to get 60,' he said, before starting the lesson with the memorable words: 'Forget that skinless haddock is king in West Yorkshire and you'll be bankrupt in three days.'

I encountered the same sense of skill and delight in good food and cooking, when a ridiculous row blew up in Rotherham over mothers passing fast food to their children through the fence of Rawmarsh high school during break. The roof fell in briefly, with Jamie Oliver and whatnot weighing in to condemn supposed trash food, when in truth the real issue was whether high school pupils were better kept on campus during break or allowed a little more freedom. But one man who wasn't happy was Keith Allgood who ran the local chip shop. 'Let Jamie Oliver come here and tell me this is junk food,' he instructed me, waving a spatula with beef dripping still glistening on the end. The wall behind him, papered with certificates for gold-star fish and quality spuds, underlined his point. His helpings were very big though, I tentatively suggested. But for many, the north is appealing because of just that – the difficulty we have with the concept of nouvelle cuisine. There are plenty of cutting edge restaurants in the three regions, such as Paul Heathcote's in Preston, Anthony Flynn's in Leeds and Winteringham Fields at Winteringham in south Humberside which saw Germain and Annie Schwab reach the critics' stratosphere before selling up. But as a general rule, size matters.

Some years ago, there was a competition for a giant statue to welcome trains coming into Leeds from the south. It achieved notoriety because the winner was an ominous-looking giant made of bricks, which the city disliked and rejected, even though the sculptor was Antony Gormley. Alas, he had not sorted out his ideas to the level of inspiration shown soon afterwards in Gateshead's *Angel of the North*. But the real story, although almost entirely unwritten, was that the brick man never actually won the competition. It came second. Most votes went to an enormous teapot, tilted and constantly pouring a stream of brown-dyed water into an equally vast cup.

Sadly, this was disqualified as a potential distraction to train drivers, who might have reverted to 125mph mode through Hunslet's crowded network of tracks, inspired by the thought of getting home for a tea of their own. It was absolutely in the spirit of northern hospitality, as exemplified by the biggest meal ever eaten in Britain,

Magna science centre's magnificence in the former Templeborough steelworks, Rotherham DON MCPHEE

The oldest sweetshop in England, based in Pateley Bridge, North Yorkshire, since 1827
CHRISTOPHER THOMOND

Retired dockers watch an unemployment demonstration in Liverpool, 1976

Steam returns to Ribblehead viaduct on the Settle-Carlisle railway in 1986
DENIS THORPE

Antony Gormley's rusted Angel by the A1 Great North Road in Gateshead has done wonders for the image of the north MURDO MACLEOD

The great north link, the M62, winds over Pennine moors CHRISTOPHER THOMOND

Old mine workings at Nenthead in the North Pennines, a landscape which inspired many poems by WH Auden DON MCPHEE

Still frying, in Yeadon, West Yorkshire

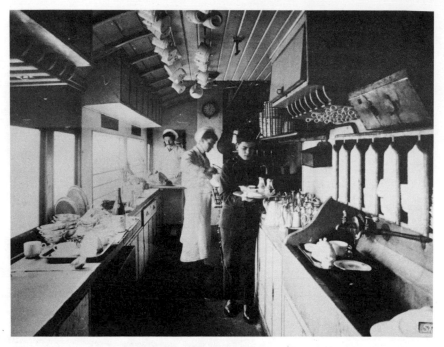

Great Northern Railway dining car, 1907

which was of course laid on in Yorkshire. Known as the great feast of Cawood, it was a two-fingers at the south, organised in 1466 by Richard Neville, the 16th Earl of Warwick, who is known to history as Warwick the Kingmaker. The excuse was the enthronement of his brother George as Archbishop of York but the real motive was to outdo the coronation feast held in London five years earlier. It succeeded, thanks to 104 oxen, six wild bulls, 1,000 muttons, 304 veals, 304 porks, 400 swans, 2,000 geese, 1,000 capons, 104 peacocks, 400 mallards and teals, 204 cranes, 204 kids, 2,000 chickens, 4,000 pigeons, 4,000 rabbits and 25,000 gallons of wine. There was a great deal more if you include the medieval equivalent of canapés, starters and puddings, but you will have to go to the Ferry Inn at Cawood to see the full menu which they display proudly alongside their own list of filling food.

Size mattered, too, when trains in Britain introduced dining cars and the first service ran between Leeds and London in 1879. The Great Northern Railway advised customers that they could leave home after a put-you-on snack to avoid rumbling tummy, in time to catch the train for a full breakfast followed by morning coffee and cakes, arriving in London in time for the business lunch which was assumed to be the reason for their trip. The return was timed to give them afternoon tea followed by a three course dinner, returning them home for a light supper before bed. Covering the recreation of this service on its 120th anniversary in 1999 was probably the most enjoyable job I have ever done.

In the same generous spirit, I was served lunch at the inaugural Yorkshire pudding birthday lunch in 1988 at Hull, where all four courses were variants on the famous but filling dish, which was said to be 241 that year, based on its first mention in print in Hannah Glasse's *The Art of Cookery Plain and Easy*. Geoff Barry, one of the organisers, confided to me, 'We haven't found a way of drinking Yorkshire Pudding yet', but they were clearly intending to. In the meantime we made the best of it with another fine northern consumable, Lindisfarne mead from Holy Island.

I have had similar combinations over the Pennines, where the famous black pudding expertise centred on Bury goes nicely with a Benny and Hot, the combination of Benedictine and hot water which soldiers from Burnley and Accrington brought back as an acquired taste from the first world war trenches, where it helped them to survive. There are still years when Lancashire takes over three quarters of Britain's Benedictine sales for this niche but extremely loyal market. The black puddings also have the blessing of the demanding guardians of French cuisine. The best known of the county's many experts, Andrew Holt of the Real Lancashire Black Pudding Co. in

Rossendale is a Chevalier de L'Ordre du Goute-Boudin Noir and his puddings have repeatedly won gold medals and the Grand Prix d'Excellence National at the Concours International du Meilleur Boudin in the French offal shrine of Mortagne-au-Perche. In 2006, he took the European Champion prize at another concours (du Meilleur Boudin Noir ou Blanc) in Belgium, and the Dutch Chevaliers du Goute-Andouilles de Jargot have also enrolled him in their ranks. Try his black pudding pancakes with bacon and custard cream or, if you do not eat meat, the vegetarian black pudding with a veggy casserole. Vegetarian black pudding? Indeed. As Holt explains, an awful lot of lovely ingredients go into black pudding – spices, herbs, pearl barley, onion, rusk, oatmeal – and they still taste good if you remove the blood and pork back-fat. A Benny and Hot would go nicely with this, but if you prefer something milder, Lancashire still has a handful of temperance bars serving sarsaparilla, notably Fitzpatrick's Herbal Health in Rawtenstall.

I am getting carried away, but perhaps that's easy to do in the north because of the proverbial friendliness which you encounter everywhere. Well, not quite. Sometimes silence is tactically deployed as a response to cheerful greetings, in the tradition of seeing all and hearing all but saying nowt. And it is easy for southern fragility to be upset by plain-speaking, if this is misinterpreted as being rude. I was once told by some British Asian friends how uncomfortable they had felt when they visited an isolated pub in the Pennines, and the few people drinking there swivelled round to stare and fell silent. 'Unnerving,' I agreed, 'but that's often happened to me too.' It will do, initially, to any unfamiliar face. Remember the opening scenes, filmed in Wharfedale, of *An American Werewolf in London*.

I never found London unfriendly myself, during 12 years of living there, and it is difficult to think of geographical or cultural reasons

Contemporary fabrics at Hopton Mill, Mirfield

why northern bosoms should warm more readily than those in the capital. Except one. There's almost always less rush up here, and more time. A smile will usually get a response even in London, although the sense of uneasiness – that fleeting expression saying 'Madman? Rapist?' – is much more common there. In the north, you are far more likely to get an added 'Now then' or 'How do?' – or in my case, a 'very well – and you?' because of the lastingly posh way I apparently mangle and extend the simple greeting 'Hiya' into what sounds like 'How-are-you?' The difference in pace is that, up here, we seem to be sure of what we're doing most of the time and concentrate on gently getting there, without a lot of faff and fuss. This is born of experience which leads in turn to comfortable expectations. When we go to the swimming baths, or a local attraction or a favourite picnic spot, we know that they are unlikely to be crowded, that we'll get a seat on the train or bus (except on the Airedale commuter lines) or find somewhere to park.

One caution needs adding. When we moved from London, there was something of a miniature influx of southerners to the north, attracted by bargain house prices compared with London and the nebulous phrase 'quality of life.' The short-lived nickname 'southeys' was even suggested by the Yorkshire branch of the Institute of Public Relations after it discovered (confirming the darkest suspicions of northerners about PR people) that a third of its members were recent refugees from down south. On cue, they all gushed about the marvellous facilities, shorter queues and northern equivalents of almost everything in London with the bonus that there was less competition, frustration and delay involved. When I light-heartedly wrote an article explaining that the one sacrifice we had made in leaving Chiswick was losing a supermarket which sold nasturtium flowers as a salad item, readers in both Leeds and Manchester ticked me off and gave me branches of Sainsbury's which supplied them,

Cumbrian fleeces insulate attics and make floor tiles

with much less waiting-time at the till. I have never actually eaten a nasturtium flower, but if you want to, the north can sell you them; and thanks to the cosmopolitan northerners whom I hail in Chapter 7, you can buy almost anything else edible as well.

Other readers meanwhile pointed out that all these joys were fine and dandy for an affluent incomer such as myself, but life in the north wasn't – and isn't – like that for everybody. There are also particular circumstances, and not just in the north, where an influx of wealth creates local inflation and shoulders out local people who would otherwise have found work on their doorstep and affordable homes. The pioneering decision of the Yorkshire Dales national park to limit the sales of newly built houses to local people only is a welcome attempt to deal with this intractable effect of market forces. But overall, history shows again and again how a welcome to outsiders brings new energy. My main hope for this book may sound narrow: encouraging movers and shakers to remain, return or move up here for the first time. But it would do a powerful lot of good.

Because doing things, making them, inventing them, selling them – the whole of that busy culture is another pillar of the north. Soon after we moved to Leeds, I took my lawnmower to a one-man outfit with a single line in Yellow Pages who operated from a lock-up garage in Yeadon. On the next unit, nailed to an unpainted and generally grotty-looking door, was a worn sign saying 'Woodcarver'. 'Your neighbour,' I asked the mower-mender. 'Do you think he would be able to knock me up a garden gate?' I had in mind one with a few extra bit-bats, to match the carved roundels on the bargeboards of our Victorian house. 'Ay,' said the man, after one of those contemplative silences mentioned above. 'He might. But he mostly does church organs and reproduction old musical instruments. You know, from mediaeval times. He sells them all over the world.'

The exchange could have taken place in Birmingham, the traditional workshop of the world, or indeed in one of those small businesses that populate the railway arches of London. But I have come to revel in the extraordinary range of products used worldwide which carry a specifically northern tag. There was Mikhail Gorbachev on TV at the height of glasnost, and what was the label on his suit? It was made by tailors down the road in Leeds. Soon after, I interviewed a textile man who wove racing cars at Summit – the mill village at the top of the Pennines where the Yorkshire and Lancashire trams met after the long haul from Halifax and Rochdale, but only at a distance. As if it were Checkpoint Charlie in the days of divided Berlin, passengers had to walk 50 yards between the white rose and red rose stops. Wove racing cars? Yes, the process was similar to the manufacture of glass fibre but with a superstrong fabric. The firm used a similar process to weave bullet-proof body armour for the police.

Making things remains central to the northern spirit. The tradition developed here from the Industrial Revolution onwards for reasons which have been explained exhaustively in thousands of books, and sedulously passed on: among them sheep farming, water power, the relative absence of feudal landowners and the exclusion of non-conformists from the professions and universities so that they directed their energies towards business. The result has been inventiveness on a scale that continues to defy undercutting by foreign goods which are much cheaper but still obliged to play catch-up when it comes to quality and niche markets. Products change, and many of today's are smaller, cleaner and less obvious. Instead of battleship-sized works in the cities, we have hi-tech laboratory clusters in otherwise quaint spots such as Boroughbridge, which has also signed up to two regeneration projects run by the regional development agency, Yorkshire Forward. One is the Renaissance town status which brought Will Alsop to

Barnsley. At Boroughbridge it triggers extra government start-up funds and business advice. The other is a youth scheme called iTown MyTown which has sent junior video teams and podcasters fanning out over the Lower Ure valley, making programmes and practising their IT. There is a similar hive of new technology at Shipley, where the Scott Sociable motorbike and sidecar was made in the 1930s, and William Spooner, son of the famous Oxford professor who created the spoonerism, invented the tumble dryer after noting how windy weather speeded up drying on local washing lines. Today, the town houses Pace Technology, which was early in the field in making satellite TV decoders, and has maintained its edge. Nearby are the offices of Filtronic, set up by a Leeds University professor, David Rhodes, and a specialist in microwave communication. Microchips earn as much and often more than molten steel; what has not changed is the inherited imagination and zeal.

Styal water wheel runs again in Cheshire

British Aerospace, high-tech leaders in the north

When Daniel Defoe travelled through the north in 1725 he was struck at how 'The country appears busy, diligent and even in a hurry of work,' and this perceptive comment should have equal billing with the far-more-emphasised northern dramas of exploitation, slumps and industrial unrest. I have toured dozens of factories and workshops across the region in the last 30 years, from Fisherman's Friend in Fleetwood to British Aerospace at Brough on Humberside, and never left without warming to the enthusiasm and involvement people have with any 'making' sort of work. At a younger age, I was struck by how often I was invited in to people's homes when I canvassed for my father as Liberal MP for the textile and engineering towns of the Colne valley, and was honoured to be shown a miniature steam locomotive or a beautifully carved welsh dresser which the householder had made – after getting home from paid work.

It's Adam's curse. We're just not happy being idle; but to make work possible, manufacturing also needs capital and leadership by people who are ready to take risks. As I write, the world is being shaken by one of capitalism's inevitable convulsions. The risk takers went too far and the cord of faith on which the whole system depends snapped, leaving people and firms dangling helpless, when a few months' more confidence might have seen them to safety. The north has been through this before, and it needs to maintain its tradition of picking things up again.

Victor Watson, the most successful chairman of the mighty northern enterprise, Waddington's, the British manufacturers of Monopoly, recalls how less than six months lay between the company and the receiver in the 1920s slump. 'It was difficult to pay the first week's wages, suppliers would not send goods without cash and there were a number of customers who could only be classed as extremely doubtful payers.' In the same pickle, the Scott family who ran a textile mill in Bradford put all their assets on the line when bankruptcy was a whisker away in the 1930s. The managing director Derek Scott accepted personal instead of limited liability to reassure creditors, selling his Dales cottage and putting his home on the market. He and his family then spent the worst weekend of the crisis repainting the works, after factory inspectors called and added to the stress by ordering that this be done.

Both firms survived, and it has been a pleasure for me that for most of my time as a northern reporter, a chauvinistic investment operation called the Yorkshire Unit Trust, confined to shares of companies based in the county, has outperformed the *Financial Times* Stock Exchange Index. And that's another of the northern virtues: local pride that creates a feeling of place so pronounced that towns and villages can take on the air of individual principalities. I remember finding one miniature realm which actually called itself a kingdom – Joseph's Little Kingdom, or the hamlet of Wilshaw in the Summer Wine country of Holmfirth. Joseph Hirst was a Victor Watson in his day, a small-scale Victorian textile manufacturer who dominated his Pennine pond but did so on the Aristotelian principles of the enlightened ruler. Still today his bust beams cordially from the entrance to St Mary's church, which he built along with houses and a school, rather than aggrandising his own home or holidaying on the Riviera as his business prospered. I got to know his great-great-grandson Tom Kirby whose family still lived at the time in Joseph's house, Wilshaw Villa, and who seemed to have inherited a similar energy and free spirit. He got fed up with his initial job as a tax inspector and joined the model war games producers, Games Workshop, whose stores in British towns and cities are usually full of young enthusiasts battling out scenes from fantasy worlds, peopled by the company's Warhammer goblins and elves, on vast layouts.

Tom led a management buyout in 1991 and is now chairman of the firm which earned more than £117 million last year.

At the Bradford *Telegraph & Argus* I made another friend from a similar northern background, a reporter called Richard Hainsworth, whose family cloth firm continues to flourish in Farsley in spite of the long and much-documented troubles of the British textile industry. It does so because of episodes such as this: after prospering cosily for years in markets such as military uniforms, with large government contracts which may not have been as tightly drawn as small private ones, the good times threatened to end. But colour TV had just come in, and one of the directors was a snooker player who realised the implications for his game. It was never broadcast in black-and-white for obvious reasons. Colour changed that and the epic dramas from the Crucible theatre in Sheffield hugely popularised the game. Hainsworth's got in there quickly with a new line in billiard cloth whose nap was so short, dense and smooth that the BBC made a documentary about it. Hainsworth's won orders for so much that a boy at my sons' primary school, whose father worked for the firm, invariably came to fancy dress parties as Robin Hood, dressed head to toe in billiard green. Their latest line is woollen coffins

You could write a book about Hainsworths' inventiveness alone and indeed historian Ruth Strong has done so, listing an extraordinary portfolio of specialised textile applications which the company has at one time or another acquired. I will mention just one because it makes the point so succinctly: in 1982 they bought L.Harwood & Co of Cleckheaton and Mytholmroyd whose biscuit cloth serviced three completely different markets. An absorbent baize, it got its common name as an effective wrapper of biscuits; soaked in synthetic resin, it is a matchless polisher of stainless steel, and finally dyed, cut and pressed it forms the punching cloths for piano keys. Recession could affect all three uses but it is far more likely that one at least will remain buoyant. In the next chapter, we will see the disastrous consequences of large-scale dependence on one trade.

Hard times also stimulate inventiveness, like the initiative of the electric toaster makers Morphy Richards, who discovered a market for one of their byproducts – 3,000 slices of toast discarded every day by their factory in Swinton after being used to test each toaster before it was packed. For many years a weekly skipful of everything from underdone brown wheatgerm to burnt white thinslice went to a local pig farmer. In 1987 the firm put the contract out to tender and got an excellent price. Staff were not deprived either. They were still entitled to eat as much as they wanted, although the managing director James Cadman told me: 'There's always plenty left.' Fields alongside the river Wharfe between Otley and Wetherby are meanwhile fertilised with gold, in the form of the nation's withdrawn banknotes. Millions of ex-pounds are mashed up with agricultural chemicals in a disused quarry near Leeds. They call it Nutramulch.

Involvement in this tradition of making things, and finding new things to make when the market for old ones collapses, has always encouraged an imaginative side in those involved. My whole theme of a partial view overwhelming the complete one applies here forcefully. The satanic mills have always had angelic design departments with staff as knowledgeable about colourways, fabrics and the history of art as any of the artists and designers they commissioned. It is not through coincidence that the Bankfield museum in Halifax has one of Britain's finest collections of embroidery; and one of the proud treasures in the Bradford archives is a full series of *The Heaton Magazine*, produced to exceptionally high standards by people working in the textile and allied trades who lived in the city's Heaton suburb. It was the place to live in Bradford for much of the 20th century, and

The gentle Summer Wine landscape of Holmfirth

still retains some cachet through inevitable misunderstandings down south when former pupils, including three of my cousins, say that they were at Heaton school, using the locally-dropped 'H'.

The magazine was meticulously printed by more craftsmen from another outwardly severe northern works, the specialists Lund Humphries who produced wonderful catalogues for Sotheby's and books for the fine art world where absolute colour accuracy was essential. I remember interviewing a member of the firm in the colour chemistry department at Bradford University, where it was difficult not to be distracted by the internal plumbing between laboratories which used heavy-duty glass pipes. They ran like rainbows with yellow, green, purple, orange and red. My parents had a talented friend called Michael Scott who was a virtuoso in this world, a man of great artistic talent and sensitivity who in the end sadly took his own life. His workday world appeared to be anything but artistic and sensitive, a big mill off the Wakefield Road out of Bradford. But like all textiles, this business required artistic knowledge and craftsmanship, and in Michael it spilled over with exuberance. He was a devotee of postal art, which is essentially what its name suggests, and on holiday once in Barcelona, my wife and I noticed that a postal art exhibition was on at the Museum of Contemporary Art. Sure enough, there were tiny, surrealist letters and drawings done by Michael and exchanged with fellow devotees across the world. For so long as he was involved, Bradford's annual festival had a contemporary edge which any time-travelling Futurist or Dadaist would have recognised.

An even more contrasting example of mighty works and delicate, sensitive humanity took place in the wild upper valley of the river Nidd, where three stupendous stone structures hold back Gouthwaite, Angram and Scar House reservoirs to guarantee our water supplies. Just the rollcall of names is solid enough, but the dams which carry them are huge, squat, unbreachable barriers. Yet look at the sketching notebooks of David Rose, the engineer who built Scar House, marshalling 600 navvies for 15 years from 1921 in an operation that meant building an entire railway line and temporary village in the dale. His drawings show marvellously deft line and a sympathy with the characters of the men, working with pickaxe and shovel or collecting their pay at the end of the week. With watercolour, he captured the essence of the lonely landscape which so many visitors feel but are challenged to describe. The instinctive, instant nature of his work is shown by touches like a brushflick of ultramarine left in error on a grey cloud. Rather than spoiling the effect, it shows the lack of polishing and cleaning up afterwards which makes his record of these huge permanent engineering works so delicate, and real.

Lastly, there was and there remains a less physical division in the north between wealth and poverty. It is there, and it has worsened in recent years with the growth of gated communities and unjustified fear of 'the other', partly in response to the way that the media's traditional battery of crime and misery now operates 24 hours and keeps a permanent record on the internet. To escape this, I sometimes drive over Eccleshill to Bradford and stop to look at the magnificent panorama of Manningham seen from the other side of the valley of the Bradford beck. It is a monument to social inclusion in stone.

JB Priestley was for once comprehensively wrong when he wrote in *English Journey* in 1934: 'If, having made some lucky gambles in wool, you made a fortune there and determined to retire and set up as an English gentleman, you never stayed in Bradford, where everyone was liable to be sardonic at your expense, but bought an estate a long way off, preferably in the south.' No you did not. You stayed nearby and built decent housing for your workers on your doorstep. You got involved, paying for a library – John Rylands in Manchester, an art gallery, lido and botanical gardens – the Listers in Bradford, or a park with tearooms in the mansion and an excursion boat zooming around an enormous lake powered by an aircraft propeller – John Barran in Leeds.

The prosperous did not usually stay in the heart of the city, although wealthy Liverpudlians were to be found in Hope Street well into the 20th century. But they were close by. In Manchester, the likes of CP Scott, who owned the *Manchester Guardian* as well as editing it, stayed within cycling distance of the office, in a house in Didsbury which is now Manchester University's vice-chancellor's home. The shining ones who dwelt in Leeds' Georgian Park Square upped and moved only just over a mile to what became known as 'New Leeds' in Chapeltown, where large mansions remain lining wide streets with plentiful trees. That area's fortunes changed over the years but the townscape did not and when there was trouble in the 1990s, and my own paper inaccurately headlined a piece 'The

David Hockney's Saltaire stamps

meanest streets in Britain', there was justified local outrage. The streets were not mean in any social sense, with community feeling bubbling out and spilling downhill into Sheepscar and Woodhouse; but neither were they physically. The pleasant urban geometry of the Victorians' avenues, leading up to Potternewton (or Potty) Park was and still is intact.

The most impressive refutation of Priestley, however, is the Manningham hillside as seen from Eccleshill, which soothes me in times of depression about social divides. There are grades of housing, clear as the coloured keys of a xylophone, but look how close they are together. Immediately below Lister's cavernous velvet mill are several terraces of back-to-backs, built of the same honey-coloured stone as the huge industrial masterpiece. Then come small 'throughs', terrace houses with a tiny front garden and a yard at the back. Then larger ones, with a garden back as well as front. Then larger ones still, and finally, in the two terraces before you reach Lister Park, very large semis, where management from the velvet works lived. The Cunliffe-Listers, it is true, did not build their own mansion in the city, preferring Wensleydale. But an even greater magnate did. Sir Titus Salt's home, Crow Nest Park, was up a leafy lane alongside the river Aire, where Bradford rowing club now practices and holds its annual regatta in between kingfisher flights. He could walk to his alpaca mill at Saltaire, an even larger edifice than Lister's, and the surrounding model village which together are now a World Heritage site. In turn, you can make the same walk in reverse today, ending at the atmospheric ruins where Salt once entertained royalty.

Salt was the son of a modestly successful woolman, but made his own fortune by buying a warehouse in Liverpool full of alpaca fleeces, which had been rejected by other textile manufacturers as too coarse to weave. His experiments gave us mohair, still as desirable as it was when Salt introduced his first batches to the market. But Saltaire is his more famous legacy, along with its associated social reforms. He promoted these with an energy which came, in part, from living so close to his mill and village that he could see the improvements happening and enjoy their benefits himself. He reduced the horrendous noise by placing machinery shafts beneath the mill floors. Pioneering dust extractors were installed in the weaving sheds and every chimney was fitted with a Rodda smoke burner, a new device which re-burned the smoke and soot from the boilers' fuel to reduce pollutants. By modern lights, much of what Salt did was paternalistic, although he was a radical supporter of the Chartists and adult suffrage and the first employer in Bradford to reduce the working day to 10 hours. But he lived on the spot and could be challenged (as he was, on several occasions, over his refusal to allow Saltaire to have a pub). The same was true of the Milligan, Briggs and Ripley families, all textile titans in Bradford, none of whom moved further away than Rawdon where the spires and turrets of some of their fanciful mansions can still be seen poking out of Cragg Wood from the trains between Skipton and Leeds. Ripley also copied Salt on a modest scale by building Ripleyville for his millworkers on a site off Manchester Road now occupied by blocks of council flats. A 1960s mural in one of them commemorates his largesse. Look at the Ackroyds and Crossleys of Halifax, too. The model village of Ackroydon still thrives, albeit now in owner-occupation, as do the mansions of the Crossleys, close to the People's Park which they gave to Halifax, and their model village of Copley. The Crossleys were unusual only in not tagging their good works with wordplay on their name.

They also win my personal prize for loyalty to place, regardless of wealth or position, and the strength it gives to any society. Edward Crossley's refusal to leave Halifax, where he was both mayor and one of the local Liberal MPs, cost him the hobby to which he was devoted, studying the rest of the universe at night. Although the Yorkshire town was in every way his world, he liked to reflect on others through a series of ever more powerful telescopes, culminating in a 36-inch whopper installed in 1885, which was the largest of its kind in the world. Crossley was delighted and used the telescope to photograph stars too distant and faint to be seen through its lens with just the eye. But he was fighting a losing battle against pollution of Halifax's air by smoke from the mill chimneys, including his own. He presented both the telescope and the revolving dome which he had built to house it to the Lick Observatory on Mount Hamilton in California, where it is known as the Crossley Reflector and became famous for discovering two of Jupiter's smaller moons.

Beat that? I think you can, with an academic project in more recent years which puts the seal on this devotion to place. One of the delights of exploring the region is to see how the buildings reflect the

Guardian of northern principles: CP Scott

local geology; in Cumbria's Vale of Eden, stonework is warm and red, while along the limestone scarp from Doncaster to north of York, buildings such as Conisbrough Castle and York Minster glow white. But the most spectacular identification of people with place is to be found in an obscure-sounding book called *The Built Stone Heritage of Leeds*, by a D-Day paratrooper called Francis Dimes, who became a geologist and recruited an academic colleague, Murray Mitchell, to help him track down the origins of all the city centre's stone.

Thus we learn that McDonald's burger bar in Briggate is faced with St John's, or Silver Moonlight travertine from a quarry at Sierra di Rapolano near Siena in central Italy. Burger King, a short walk north, uses slabs of a gneissic granite known as Juparana, which is quarried in Brazil. If you want to go somewhere different for a coffee after your fast food, Starbucks on the corner of Commercial and Albion streets has three types of stone from the same quarry, much nearer home, at Arthington beside the river Wharfe. The best grade is at eye-level, the second on the first floor and the cheapest, down in the basement and up by the eaves.

The book is a wonderful compendium of detailed information, from evocative quarry names – Idle, Bursting Stones, Roo – to the rare distinction of the Slug and Lettuce pub – like Starbucks, a former bank – being the only building in the whole of Leeds to use oolitic Gloucester limestone, perhaps because it weathers to an orange as vivid as the colour of double Gloucester cheese. Dimes was previously curator of the Geological Museum's collection of building stones in South Kensington. His absorption in his adopted city is testimony to the power, today as in the past, of the north's sense of place.

4
The Grumpiness Factor

*'You cannot be absolutely dumb when you live
with a person, unless you are an inhabitant of the
north of England.'*
Ford Madox Ford, *The Good Soldier*

We speak as we find in the north, so I won't fanny around. There are too many orange-tanned women up here and far too many owners of four-by-four pretend Jeeps with personalised numberplates. I know very nice people who fit into both categories but I wish that they didn't. I'm not properly qualified to rule on the fashion status of orange skin and the merits or otherwise of the Wilmslow look, although I'm glad that I don't myself live in a town which has 'A' streets and 'B' streets, so rigid is the pecking order of Cheshire social status. Apparently the pyramid peaks with a slender summit of those who get invited to garden parties at the Bromley-Davenports in Capesthorne Hall. A woman from Wilmslow told me this on holiday in Corfu shortly after I'd encountered a friendly family splashing about in Kalami bay. 'They're staying at a villa on the peninsula and guess what they're called,' I told her. 'Bromley-Davenport.' Her face was a picture.

But I do know that quite a few women friends of mine look at themselves nervously in the mirror before paying a return visit to their native London or points south. 'Am I a bit too … northern?' they wonder, tremulously. In other words, are they bedizened and bedazened like an 'A' street Wilmslow woman, or one from Wetherby or parts of Gosforth in Newcastle, about to embark in warpaint on a night out? It's all about not flaunting and – although I would never presume to make judgments on the matter – what the south calls good taste.

But there are much more seriously undesirable aspects to the north, which you can discover if you turn off the M1 or A1M in South Yorkshire or the great north road in Northumberland. They are not bad in many senses; you will find local people almost unfailingly warm and welcoming – abetted in parts of South Yorkshire with the

Facework. One of the toughest jobs in the world

thee-ing and thou-ing which has the intimate feel of tu-toying in France. But the statistics of poverty and deprivation are a blot on the whole country. They date from the crushing of the miners' strike of 1984-5 and the subsequent loss of 220,000 mining jobs and a further 135,000 in manufacturing and associated trades.

I take these figures not from some Scargillite faction but the authoritative Audit Commission, which presents them in the context of excellent recovery work undertaken in the 25 years since the catastrophe. In some ways, the disaster has started to heal as many previous slumps and large-scale bankruptcies have done in the past. Walk down Swaledale on the moor-tops and you will see the moonscape left by a lead-mining industry of which absolutely nothing remains, apart from a rusting stone-crushing machine which I was pleased to see, when I marched past on the coast-to-coast walk, was made in Leeds.

Recovery takes a long time, especially when the scale of employment has been so huge. Two examples of this stick in my mind because of that. The first was the one I have recounted in Chapter 1, of taking a work experience student to see the last shipyard on the Wear in Sunderland in 1988. Neither of us could believe that such a gigantic collection of buildings, employing so many people, would be razed by the end of the year. Next, it was quite extraordinary to visit Consett a year or so after the closure of its mighty steelworks, and find an enormous sandy-coloured wasteland where the furnaces had been, and the metalwork for Blackpool Tower and Britain's nuclear submarine fleet forged. Out of a working population of 30,000 in the County Durham town, 9,000 lost their jobs in 1981. By 1990, there were still 3,400 on the dole and the new industries, although prospering, were minnows by comparison with British Steel. The best-known and most frequently described in media visits to Consett

Welsh ponies, once a staple of the mines

was Derwent Valley Foods, whose most successful line was potato crisps branded as Phileas Fogg – Fine Foods From Around the World, after Jules Vernes' hero in *Around the World in Eighty Days*. There was something a little science fiction-like about comparing a 10 tonne component for a nuclear sub with a wafer thin curl of cooked manioc flour, flavoured with prawn and marketed as a java cracker.

However weird the new way of working, though, at least Sunderland and Consett got cracking on it. After the closure of the northern pits from the mid-1980s onwards, there was a different and very depressing legacy. Michael O'Higgins, chairman of the Audit Commission, summed it up for me in March 2009 at the Keepmoat Stadium in Doncaster, home of the Championship side Doncaster Rovers and, more appealing to my mind, the Doncaster

Belles, one of the best women's football teams in Britain. Failure by the then government to act promptly to bring hope to the shattered communities led, he said, to a disastrous 'culture of worklessness.' The well-documented saga of hopeless, drug-afflicted lethargy that beset many mining communities – young people as well as miners thrown suddenly on to the dole – was the direct result. Again, this is not some National Union of Mineworkers apparatchik speaking, but the head of the independent accountants who work for all of us to check that the government is getting value for money and doing an efficient job.

Even in 2009, the rate of real unemployment (which is to say, those on invalidity benefit for being medically unable to work, often for psychological reasons, as well as those on the straightforward dole) is 16 per cent in the former Durham pit village of Easington. The share of regional populations living in the most deprived 20 per cent of council wards sees the north win gold, silver and bronze with 37 per cent for the north-east, 33 per cent for the north-west and 28 per cent for Yorkshire and the Humber. London comes in fourth, at 27 per cent.

But the Audit Commission's report on coalfield regeneration, *A Mine of Opportunities*, makes another interesting point: the number of the new jobs in ex-mining areas that have been taken by people coming in from outside. The report estimates that Britain's former coalfields had 150,000 more jobs by 2006 than in 1998, but 38 per cent of these had gone to new residents. The stubborn difficulty, it suggested, is with local people who have not taken the same opportunities.

There is an economic reason for that, although it is not the whole story. Local people were the ones who prospered on the relatively high pay rates in mining, and the associated benefits from free fuel to the wealth of assistance offered by the NUM. Successor industries have not been in the same league, as a survey of redundant miners carried out in 1994 by the Coalfields Communities Campaign, a consortium of local councils, discovered. A lot of attention was given to its findings in Grimethorpe, the pit village near Barnsley whose coking works were for years a landmark on the M1, opposite the turn-off to the Henry Moore sculpture park at Bretton Hall. Grimey was also made famous by the film *Brassed Off*, based on the colliery's celebrated band (which, like the one in the film, has survived and even retained a sponsor from within the industry, Richard Budge's mining firm Powerfuel, which bought and reopened Hatfield Main pit in 2006).

The band was fine, but the working community was not. Two years after Grimethorpe's closure, 44 per cent of former miners were still out of work, which is what attracted headlines. It was a shocking figure in itself, but made gloomier by the fact that the pit was one of the later ones to close and a reasonable number of new industries had established themselves nearby since the 1984-5 strike. The survey's other figures were instructive in this respect. Only a handful of the 46 per cent of ex-miners who had new jobs were earning the same or more than the average weekly pit wage of £217. For those with jobs at new firms, the average fall was £65 and for those who had used their redundancy to set up on their own, it was £70. The figures were made real for me when I interviewed one of the men who had started his own business. Malcolm Hanson was bravely running a one-man printing outfit in one of the classrooms of the former primary school at Brampton Bierlow, beside the remains of the Cortonwood colliery whose closure had triggered the disastrous strike. He was making a go of it, just, but earning nothing like his former wage and had been obliged to remortgage his house.

Famous for camaraderie, mining could be lonely too

Shift end at Deepdale colliery, Co Durham, 1964

I call the strike 'disastrous' not just because of its outcome. Its conduct was an example of the unappealing side of the north, one described 140 years earlier in Charlotte Brontë's *Shirley*. It is well worth reading the whole of the chapter entitled 'Mr Yorke' for her perceptive analysis of the dark counterpart to her eponymous hero Hiram Yorke's great northern virtue, an independent mind. While she praises this spirit, she deplores what she called his 'want of veneration.' She shows a now old-fashioned but very real distaste for the way the sturdy millowner sneered at the gentry and church hierarchy. And in her hands, Yorke's chippiness went a lot further than that and in a much less attractive way. He was unwilling to listen to or even acknowledge any contrary point of view. This applied particularly if it was coming from anyone whom he suspected of feeling superior to him – to use another old-fashioned phrase, 'giving themselves airs.' He could be indulgent, kind and fatherly, certainly, but only to those who were very definitely inferior to him.

There have been many Mr Yorkes but the one I want to direct your attention to is Arthur Scargill, who personifies to many the crudely belligerent and apparently deaf sort of northerner. This is unfair, of course, and partly a result of the need of the media to simplify complicated issues and if possible present them through individuals rather than as concepts. But it is possible to deflect that sort of treatment or to encourage it, and Scargill did the latter. In his oratory, behaviour and personalising of the enemy into the rival dominant figure of Margaret Thatcher, he did nothing to discourage the 'King Arthur' legend. Indeed to this day he turns up at his desk most days in the ghostly remnant of the National Union of Mineworkers which was once his Barnsley 'castle.'

His aggressively self-righteous stance rarely slips in public, which is all the more lamentable when he has a quite different side. On the few occasions that I have met him in private, he has been as reasonable and agreeable as most superficial acquaintances, and I have seen him behave on one public platform with a masterfully persuasive style. This was at an expert inquiry into a mining accident which killed two men and Scargill appeared for the NUM to argue the case over management liability. The whole occasion was understated and discouraging to oratory. It was held on the beautiful campus donated by the chemist Jesse Boot to Nottingham University, on a spring day when the many cherry trees between the academic buildings were in bloom. The chairman was a scholarly geologist and the tragedy of the accident was in the minds of all involved. Scargill displayed tremendously impressive knowledge of his industry, in detail and depth, and although he was making a case which alleged cost-cutting by British Coal, he did so quietly and without the rancour of his strike speeches. If only, I kept thinking. If only this Scargill had been on our television sets in 1984-5, instead of the relentlessly angry and confrontational one.

The harm the latter did was to encourage the worst in everyone. The rights and wrongs of running down Britain's coalmining industry are beyond the scope of this book, but the way that debate was turned so rapidly into battle was disastrous for all concerned. Did the Conservative government provoke? If so, what more doomed response to provocation is there than to respond in kind, or worse? If Mrs Thatcher was an Iron Lady at the time, devoid of human sympathy but needing the public's, she could not have hoped for a better enemy than implacable King Arthur and his unquestioningly loyal troops.

I met the opposite in 2009 when construction workers in the 'gipsy army' of platers, welders and steel erectors which moves between contracts at large energy sector projects, were involved in a dispute at Lindsey oil refinery on the south bank of the Humber estuary. There was anger, but the strikers were keen to explain their case, describing their long apprenticeships and training and the contracting system which for years had maintained high standards of work.

I have already mentioned the old question: have you ever met a miner who wanted his sons to go down the pit? I have, but precious few. Even an acclaimed laureate of the industry such as Harold Heslop, whose descriptions of mining life in the north-east sold in their millions in the Soviet Union in its early days, called the world of coal deplorable and presented its virtues primarily as a response to dreadful conditions and harsh, implacable relations between management and men. Overwhelmingly, the reply when I asked miners about their sons was: No, never, and sometimes that was even if the lad in question wanted a career in coal. Mining has gradually become better-controlled and more automated work, with far less of the grim hacking at cramped faces of the old days. Since Richard Budge reopened Hatfield colliery in 2007, a small number of apprentices have been employed at £240 a week, which is well above average local wages; but the next generation is still steered away. In South Kirkby, just as Frickley pit prepared for its final shifts in 1993, I met a young man who was frustrated and disconsolate after doing a series of 'non-jobs' largely invented by work creation schemes. When we chatted, he was fishing about lethargically with a pole in some ponds which an environmental charity was slowly clearing of gunk.

'I want a real job like mining, not this,' he said, 'but my dad says if I ever go down the pit, he'll disown me.' His dad had of course been a miner and in common with most of his mates at Frickley, was insistent that his sons get out of it and into a wider world. The issue was and remains a tug of war. The same miners or ex-miners who took this line are often full of marvellous, heartfelt reminiscences about life underground and the camaraderie which comes from

Rough work. A miner's hands

sharing hard and sometimes dangerous work. When I visited the primary school at Frickley I found this ambiguous message being given at the earliest possible age. Children were being educated for other lives which would almost certainly take them away to college and elsewhere in the country, perhaps even abroad. The primary was even twinned with a similar-sized one in Bognor Regis. But the entry foyer which the kids scooted through between classes was dominated by an historical display about mining with actual large lumps of coal. In the playground, the children had a genuine coal-wagon to use as a climbing frame, donated by the doomed pit. I asked two small boys who were scrambling about on it: what do you want to do when you work? 'Miner,' both shot back instantly.

You have to decide in the end, and while there is no denying the body blow that the closure of the coal mines represented, nobody benefits from perpetuating a victim culture. For sanity's sake, there needs to be a time limit on savouring the wrong done to you, which involves the illusion that things recently lost were timeless, rather than being themselves replacements for something earlier, which was lost in its turn. This was a revelation to some participants on a community film-making project in Allerton Bywater, after 1,000 jobs and the last three local pits closed in the spring of 1993. Helped by Leeds University's department of community and industrial studies, the amateur film crew rapidly became very professional and in November that year, they staged a 'European premiere' for the movie, *From Green to Black and Green Again*. It told the story of how 'Alreton' in the Domesday Book had many and varied trades before the hunt for coal turned it into a pit village which many locals came to believe had never been anything else.

One of the older participants, Elsie Harris, who was 77 and high up in the cast list, told me how her grandfather had been an extremely accomplished stonedresser. Fortunately for him, the wealthy Bland family who played the part of local squires at Kippax Hall were always adding to its length, in an attempt to prevent the equally vast Wentworth Woodhouse near Rotherham from taking the title of the longest house in England (which it won in the end, when Kippax was demolished in the 1950s). There were potteries in Allerton Bywater before coal and shipbuilding and repair yards for vessels using the Aire and Calder navigation. Just down the road at Knottingley, ships launched sideways into the Aire from yards on the bank were large enough to serve on the trade runs to the United States and South America.

Dig back only two generations at Hoyland near Barnsley, too, and you discover that the feeling of permanence created around mining communities can have surprisingly shallow roots. Hoyland Silkstone pit closed in 1928 with all the disastrous effects of today but worsened by the absence of redundancy payments or the chance of transfer elsewhere. But its loss was not an entirely local disaster. The colliery was well known for employing many Lancashire miners who moved across the Pennines to find work when their own pits were closed at the end of the 19th century. The redbrick houses of Henshaw Terrace, demolished not long before the 1984-5 strike, housed so many of them that it was nicknamed Lanky Row.

Similarly, another of Hoyland's pits, Elsecar Main, employed a large number of Staffordshire miners who came north at the start of the 20th century during hard times in their own county. Far from encountering a world of socialist brotherhood, they were disliked for their supposed parsimony, which perhaps threatened the pride of Yorkshire people with their own legendary reputation for thrift. Sheila Ottley, a Hoyland printer's daughter who went to Oxford and became a schoolteacher, recalls a neighbour of her family's saying that if he was in charge, every Irishman working at Elsecar Main would have to swim home, with a Staffordshire man on his back.

There are so many other subtleties in a picture which has wrongly been painted, or rather scrawled, in black and white. When Clement Attlee's Labour government approved opencast mining in the gardens of Wentworth Woodhouse in 1946, they were astonished that the National Union of Mineworkers threatened to strike to protect what from London seemed an island of extreme aristocratic privilege. Manny Shinwell, the minister of fuel and power, had no idea that what he called 'a nobleman's palace and pleasure grounds' had been enjoyed by everyone locally for years – right up to the mansion's front door, with skating in winter on the frozen fountain ponds. Joe Hall, Scargill's predecessor as president of the Yorkshire NUM, told reporters in April 1946: 'It is sacrilege. Against all common sense. The miners in this area will go to almost any length rather than see Wentworth Woodhouse destroyed. It has taken at least a century to produce these lovely grounds and gardens. Yorkshire people cannot stand by and see it all devastated in a few weeks.' He was no defender of the almost unimaginable inequality between the Fitzwilliams and their miners, but he understood fairness, context and history.

This far from monocultural past informs and encourages people trying to turn the miserable results of the 1984-5 strike and the mass closure of pits to good account. 'No one is underestimating the problems here in finding new employment,' Anne Walker, one of the tutors from Leeds University, told the premiere audience at Allerton Bywater. 'But the film is a revelation about how green and pleasant Allerton Bywater was in the past; and how it found prosperity in ways apart from coal.' The showing was followed by others in Strasbourg and Brussels, in front of politicians with the power to release European money. It played its part in showing that life and

Concessionary coal in Ashington, Northumberland, 1982

imagination had survived the coalmining disaster and were ready for
a revival, with the help of government and EU funds.

This was a good deployment of a resource which can turn to the
bad; the strong but inward-looking spirit of communities created
and sustained by huge single industries such as steel, shipbuilding
or coal. This is often marvellously powerful and inclusive; during
the recession of 1993 I went to Partington on the flat western rim
of Manchester, where the social centre was preparing for Christmas
with traditional turkey dinners costing only £1.40 to meet a need
among the 12,000 people on the overspill estate, stretching out next
to a chemical factory and the redundant Carrington power station,
for that most basic essential, affordable hot meals. Unemployment in
Partington was 20 per cent and community workers on the ground
were tired of patronising government advice that everyone should
eat more greens. 'A figure sticks in my mind,' Tony Dobson of the
family centre run by the Children's Society told me. 'It costs £1.40 –

Old men, young women, at Durham miners' gala

the same as our Christmas dinner – to get 100 calories from celery, and only 13p to get them from biscuits.' There are proteins and vitamins to get in a proper diet too, of course, but his point went home. Partington's plight had an effect well beyond its boundaries, as a contributor of data to Sir Douglas Black's report on inequality and health, published in 1980 and revised in 1992, which the then Conservative governments disliked and did their best to sideline but could not gainsay.

In the same way, a mining village such as South Kirkby has shown the merits of optimistic, resolute community spirit in the face of catastrophe. There was a good foundation to build on in the shape of a town council which used its modest powers to the full. Although strictly only a parish authority, South Kirkby and Moorthorpe council used every penny it was legally allowed to raise to set up pre-school playgroups, lay out children's playgrounds and several sports pitches, plant hundreds of trees, turn a field into a town park and buy the site of an iron age hill fort to preserve it for posterity. The spirit of the place is personified in the character of its historian Aaron Wilkinson, who went down the pit at 14 to work as a pony driver, but was not content to limit his horizons to West Yorkshire. When he turned 21, he formed a team of acrobats with two work colleagues and toured the country with a circus. War service took him to Egypt where his curiosity led him to try a little amateur archaeology. An unusual Graeco-Roman lamp which he unearthed is now in the Museum of Alexandria.

But this enlightened use of community strength was not universal. Down the road at Royston near Barnsley, the Miners Welfare park is so called because miners took a small stop out of their wages to pay for its creation because neither the council nor management would. This was an example of the alternative power base in the coalfields. If elected bodies or large companies neglected the common welfare, the union stepped in. Miners' welfare clubs were often palatial buildings, offering a formidable range of services. Through the union families got cut-price goods including televisions, washing machines and other mod cons. It was a corporate community and flourished as such; but the seeds of disaster were there for when the good times came to an end.

Well before that happened, it became clear that other characteristics of these tight communities were going against the grain of modern times. Although they were said to rule behind the scenes with their rolling pins, in the manner of Florrie Capp or a Bamforth's postcard, women had a definite place in most mining villages, and it was an inferior one. This was true of the country generally, but it was especially marked in communities whose staple industry was an almost entirely men-only affair – the pit brow lasses who shovelled coal above ground had vanished, although it took a long time. The last two finally retired in 1972. Male bonding was also very strong in mining which required underground workers to look out for one another constantly. Women, meanwhile, took lower-paid jobs in offices, textiles or food processing. Working men's clubs barred them from voting, standing for the committee or even signing in a friend. There would frequently be rooms or bars where they were made to feel unwelcome or sometimes officially barred. Denise Parkinson, a woman brought up in this world in Barnsley, makes this point in a community-published book of local memories, *Seams of Gold*. She emphasises the dramatic change post-1985 from what she calls 'institutionalised male dominance, embedded in everyday social controls and ideologies':

'In many families in Barnsley there is a role reversal with women now the main wage earner. That has effectively cracked the glass ceiling that is inherent in a community that has been male-dominated for so long. Opportunities and support for Barnsley women who are willing to motivate themselves to gain qualifications are there in abundance. As the nature of work in Barnsley moves into areas where computing skills and education are necessary to secure well-paid jobs, women can compete on equal terms with men and finally end discrimination within the community, though there is still a long way to go.'

I quote Parkinson at length because she is a Barnsley woman from a council estate in a mining area, while I am a well-to-do man from an affluent part of Leeds. But I also recall a shocking interview with a woman studying at Northern College, a classic 'second chancer' who had wasted her schooldays. She told me how when she first took her homework back from Wentworth Castle, her (then) husband chucked it on the fire. It was ironic in the spring of 2009 to read Arthur Scargill listing the Women Against Pit Closures movement as one of triumphs of his disastrous strike. So it was; but what had happened to all that flair and energy before the crisis came? And isn't it great to see it – *pace* Denise Parkinson – now taking its rightful place in the post-coal, post-macho communities which are emerging, slowly and often painfully, as they always do from vast economic change?

Occasionally, in my *Guardian* role, I get asked to join the worthy ranks of people considered right to give out school prizes and make uplifting remarks. I enjoy this, and never more so than one summer not long after the main pit closures in South Yorkshire. The venue was the comprehensive at Maltby near Rotherham, whose pit was still working – and now is again, reopened by the private Hargreaves Group which bought it in 2007 after a decade in mothballs under British Coal. So the mining culture was still there, and indeed I was more nervous than usual because the proceedings were being watched by Sir Jack Layden, the council leader and very much an Old Labour man. But I need not have worried. As I recounted earlier, I told the students about the advantages, when seeking work, of coming from an area that outsiders perceived to be tough and character-moulding. But what struck me most was that the long file of pupils with multiple As and gold stars included girl after bright, high-aiming young girl. Dawn Collins was off to read law at Nottingham University with her straight As; Emma Wright got a cheer for getting into Oxford, and then a forgiving sigh for choosing Somerville as her college. We all knew who had been an undergraduate there. There were still more boys than girls among the prizewinners overall, just, but the battle was clearly being won.

Women are not the only inferior beings in the north's tight communities, however. They can still be no place for an outsider, still less for anyone who defied the majority. The treatment of scab workers was an offence to the very principles of community and the psychology lingers: bitterness is still stoked and resentment lives on. I have been told with pride that divisions originally created in the 1926 strike still continue, as if this were some sort of historical badge of honour, an attitude that I have only encountered elsewhere in countries crippled by resentful history, such as Ireland, Cyprus and Armenia. In early 2009, I wrote a story about the miner and the policeman seen in a moment of human contact during the 1984 siege of Orgreave coking plant caught in a Don McPhee photograph, after a BBC North producer, Lucy Smickersgill, did a brilliant job of tracking them down. There was a lot of good in this story, but one of its bad sides was the issue of scabs. The miner's widow, Pat Breeley, told me how he had given his pre-teen sons the addresses of local strike-breakers so they could smash their windows. The policeman, Paul Castle, himself the grandson of a miner from Kent, said that

Arthur Scargill in action at Warrington, 1983

the thing that sickened him and his colleagues most, and weighed against their sympathy for the embattled mining communities, was the vicious way that scabs were treated.

Anger at strike-breakers is understandable, and in a struggle on the scale of 1984-5 it was bound to be intense. But where is the understanding shown, for example, by Lee Hall in *Billy Elliot* where the talented young dancer's father goes back to work so that his son can escape this claustrophobic world and spread his wings? Casting aside all politics and imagining the miners' strike from millennia ahead, as we now view classical Greek drama, who would not accept that a scab in Edlington, the red-hot base of George Breeley's Yorkshire Main colliery strikers, must at least have had considerable courage.

And then there was the dependency, whether on the local council or the union, which was a final downside of strong communities or those in a permanent state of embattlement, as if they were Mediterranean outposts of Christian Europe against the Ottoman empire. I saw the results of this when I chaired the National Lottery charities board in Yorkshire and the Humber. We grew increasingly concerned at the way that three undoubted areas of need, the council districts of Barnsley, Doncaster and Rotherham, consistently under-performed in terms of applications. In the end, we negotiated a ring-fenced sum of money for Barnsley as an experiment and actually went touting for applicants in local pubs and supermarket car parks.

Brass for Barnsley was a success; even though some punters shied away from us as though we were mad, a stall at the 'mushroom' shelter in the middle of the town's famous market attracted customers. The council laid on an excellent launch too, which brought in 'third sector' groups who then spread the word. But throughout the exercise it was evident that a psychology had to be reversed. The community had to overturn a long, and understandable, assumption that need would be met by the mighty triumvirate of the National Union of Mineworkers, British Coal and the Labour party. All were now a shadow of their former selves; indeed British Coal no longer existed except as a property business winding up former colliery sites.

This problem was perceived, as you would expect, by the Audit Commission when it sent a team to Easington to monitor the local council's progress in dealing with the catastrophic fallout from pit closures. No one should underestimate the difficulties involved, but it is instructive that the commission's report in 2004 underlined the way that a once all-powerful, Labour/NUM authority had been forced to realise that the world of monoliths – British Coal on one side, themselves on the other – had gone. The commission said: 'The

The NUM HQ leaves London for the north, 1983

council learned that it would have to work in a mixed economy of public and private provision of services. It learned that working with partners was the only way to address the area's problems. It learned that a paternalistic approach to local people was no longer acceptable.'

Taken together, the conservatism of the coalfield communities and the truculence of the miners' leaders were a deadly combination in the aftermath of colliery closures. Enormous and expensive efforts have done much to put that right, although recovery looks very fragile in the face of the recession that followed the collapse of the banking system in 2008. But the wider danger is that the continuing hangover from the pit closures will spread more widely and encourage a victim mentality in the region as a whole; a resentful feeling that we will never get a fair deal from London.

High noon for the strike. The battle of Orgreave 1984

However understandable, this is particularly dangerous when a centralised media with already inaccurate mindsets about the regions is waiting to have its prejudices about chippy northerners confirmed. We play into their hands if we turn, as too many northerners still do, any suggestion of improvement or cheerfulness in the region into yet another ghastly southern plot.

I had an example of this in 1994 when to my great delight two sets of government statistics showed, first, that the long-standing trend of northerners migrating to the south had been reversed for the previous two years; and second, that the north had the eight lowest unemployment figures in the country. Windermere did best with 2.4 per cent, followed by Keswick, Kendal, Settle, Penrith, Malton, Northallerton and Pickering. It was only then that the south got a look-in with Winchester and Eastleigh, where unemployment stood at 3.6 per cent. Unfortunately the data was released by a (northern) firm of stockbrokers who added a come-on to whet journalists' appetites by describing this phenomenon as a 'northern playground.' On cue, I got several letters of complaint, saying that the only reason for these otherwise encouraging figures was that wealthy southerners were coming north to play.

This is my final beef with such attitudes: it is infuriating to have to concede to outsiders and critics of the region that its inhabitants can be, yes, gloomy, reticent and dour. I remember that episode in *The Railway Children*, set in the north by Edith Nesbit and filmed on the Keighley and Worth Valley railway in the Pennines. When the children go round collecting in secret for Perks the station porter, they encounter one grim old villager who says nothing for ages, a northern linguistic tactic which can be quite engaging if followed by some dry fun. Nothing like that in this case, though. Just an eventual: 'I 'ate the man.' In similar vein, my Uncle Chris draws on more than

30 years' experience as a vicar in Bradford to explain why people there never take their overcoats off. 'If it isn't raining, it soon will be,' he says. Suitably, the statue of JB Priestley outside the National Media Museum shows him clad in a large gabardine.

Part of me likes to think that the condition is especially bad on the western side of the Pennines, because the rain does fall more heavily there, however stout the denials from Manchester. For years in my early reporting career, there was a particular dismalness about that great city. Where Leeds was dry and optimistic and full of hype, Manchester seemed hurt, withdrawn and incapable of thinking that its golden years could return. There was a logic to this, because its economy had slid and slid since the great Victorian days when it almost punched its weight equally with London. But then a bang – literally, one organised by the IRA – changed all that. A lorry filled with 3,300 lb of explosives went off in Corporation Street on the mid-morning of June 15 1996, miraculously killing no one and causing only minor injuries (albeit to 206 people). It was the biggest in Britain since the second world war and it blasted Manchester not into bits, but into astonishing, galvanised, communal action. Within a decade the place was utterly, wonderfully transformed.

This episode pointed up how sapping and ultimately self-defeating the previous cast of mind in the city had been. I remember another example, from my student days, when I helped to organise exhibitions at university for the chaotic but endearing painter from Wigan, Jim (Lawrence) Isherwood. He was like a fun version of Lowry (there's another northern gloom merchant), certainly not of the same calibre but with as much experience of adversity for most of his life and less in the way of critical acclaim as a compensation in mature years. He did not mind the latter. Instead he relished the headlines which accompanied his deliberately provocative work, especially a nude of

Police and pickets' impromptu soccer, Bilsthorpe 1984

the TV campaigner Mary Whitehouse with multiple breasts which was helpfully bought by her deadly enemy, the BBC's director general Sir Hugh Greene, prompting more, massive publicity. Ishy was light-hearted, energetic, an enthusiast. But he was always accompanied by his mum, known as Mother Lily, and although ever-helpful and really a dear, she was the only person I've met who answered the anodyne query 'How are you?' by saying 'Not so good' – always – instead of the customary response, 'Not so bad.' Although not from Bradford, she always wore an overcoat and it was only when Jim's red van broke down or had punctures, which often happened, that she broke into an I-told-you-so smile, albeit one of great sweetness.

A third example, also interesting because he was an exceptionally kind and thoughtful man, was my late colleague Don McPhee, the distinguished photographer who was a Mancunian to his backbone. His response to an idea was always, initially, that it couldn't be done, wouldn't work and in any case would never get past the London newsdesk. We who knew him, happily went through a sort of social ballet, appearing to agree but gradually persisting because we knew that the grumpiness was to buy time and would dissolve. I know that I made matters worse by being annoyingly bouncy, but it was like starting a particularly tricky car. People who did not know Don, or were dealing with him over the phone or by computer from elsewhere, could be scared off and not play the necessary game.

I had occasion to ponder this towards the end of 2008 when I had to give a talk to the Wainwright Society, which is nothing to do with me but brings together enthusiasts for Alfred, the excellent but very grumpy northern fellwalker and writer. I was a bit stuck for things to talk about, since the nature of a society like this is to find out every exhaustive detail about its subject and the audience was bound to know much more than I did about AW. Rereading his work, however, and doing so alongside that of another redoubtable Lake

Gresford pit memorial near Wrexham. One of hundreds

District man, Harry Griffin, the *Guardian's* late Country Diarist, a theme came to me. Given the entrancing beauty of the Lakes and its transformative power (which both men acknowledge as affecting their lives), why are they so cross?

Wainwright is forever going on about the iniquities of modern life, yobs on the hills, unwanted wives (his own marriage being a cruel disaster), and other such subjects which the timeless glory of the fells should banish from their worshippers' minds. Harry, whom I knew well in the later of his 93 years, was almost as pessimistic although he had a lively fierceness which makes his diatribes that bit more appealing, at least to me. He was very pleasant in person, rather on Scargill lines, which came as a surprise. Having read him for many years before finally going to interview him on Kirkstone Fell for his 80th birthday, I had expected a modern Fury. He only had to meet one other walker, in his Country Diary, to embark on a Jeremiad about how the Lakes were impossibly crowded these days.

Unlike Wainwright, who wrote and drew and wrote and drew, Griffin got involved in civic affairs in Cumbria (and before that, his beloved Westmorland which he could scarcely bear to see dismantled in 1974 as a local authority). In this, he came some way towards another great pedestrian of the north, Benny Rothman, the best-known leader of the Kinder Scout mass trespass in 1932. Benny's career, in Communism, fellwalking, union shop stewardship, allotment-tending and family life, was always vigorous, forward-looking and fun. He upheld the motto of George Ward, founder of Sheffield Clarion Club (the socialist cycling group) that 'A rambler made is a man improved.' He was of a like mind with Allen Clarke, the Bolton millworker turned writer (under the pen-name of Teddy Ashton) and founder of a 'communist colony' near Blackpool, who wrote before his death in 1935 of his desire to be buried:

Where I can hear the cyclists halt
And hear the yarns they spin
And there I will rest, and watch, and bless
The sweet and jolly scene
Till the Master of Cycles bids me rise
And mount my new machine.

Only five foot tall, Rothman galvanised the Kinder trespass, and was still in vigorous but good-humoured form as the star of the 50th anniversary mass picnic when he was 71. He had to accept a wheelchair in the end, but from it he campaigned to keep a tiny suburban footpath open near his home in Cheshire, to provide neighbouring mothers with a short cut to school. He was perhaps the finest defender of our great northern, open land.

We have to accept, however, that many of those who tried to keep Rothman, and Wainwright and Griffin out were also northerners. I remember some farmers dynamiting stone at Dog Rocks on Yellow Slacks on the western edge of Bleaklow in the Dark Peak (what a litany of northen names), who responded to criticism: 'It is no one's business but our own. An Englishman's home is his castle and we intend to protect ours.' Another such was Sir John Wallace, a 19th-century landowner in the Lake District who waxed furious during a dinner at Lowther Castle about vandals who had torn a gap in one of his walls that very day. But at least he was given a magnificent come-uppance. One of his fellow guests – all solid true blues being treated by their political patron Viscount Lowther, Earl of Lonsdale – turned to him and said, as the table fell silent: 'I broke your wall down, Sir John. It was obstructing an ancient right of way and if necessary I will do it again. I am a Tory but scratch me on the back deep enough and you will find the Whig in me yet.' The guest was

William Wordsworth, and you can't do better than that. With him in mind, let us now turn to the glories of the northern countryside – and the greening of its towns.

5

The Green in the Grey

*'Certainly if I did not believe there was another world,
I would spend all my summers here, as I know no place
in Great Britain comparable to it for pleasantness.'*
John Wesley on Newcastle 1759

As anyone who has visited any of the five northern national parks can testify, the countryside between the river Trent and the Scottish border can be as gentle and pretty as anywhere that the sweet Thames runs softly. But travellers are left with a much stronger impression of larger, grander vistas: the sweep of the Pennine moors, the beetling cliffs at St Bees and Flamborough and the majestic summits of Lakeland. They are what the excitable romantic travellers of the 17th century called 'aweful', 'terrible' and 'horride' and what the rather kinder experts in art history today know as the Sublime.

Similarly, our imposing collection of stately homes in the north is generally made up of the vast, although it does include the smallest of the type in the country as well – the miniature mansion of Ebberston Hall between Scarborough and Pickering. Wentworth Woodhouse near Rotherham has the longest façade of any house in Britain, and is also the country's largest back-to-back, as the original mansion was joined by a second one, in what was then a more modern style, built directly behind it. Sir John Vanbrugh built some of his chief works in the north. He loved the wide open feel of the countryside; there is actually a village called Wideopen not far from his great mansion built for the Hastings family at Seaton Delaval in Northumberland. He himself referred to the 'tame and sneaking south', and if you visit Castle Howard in particular you will sympathise with his obituarist's emphasis on the role of the enormous in his work:

> *Lie heavy on him, Earth! For he*
> *Laid many heavy loads on thee.*

They do things differently elsewhere. When I went from Leeds as a young and impressionable newcomer to work in Bath, the most beautiful city in Britain and a place of voluptuous softness, I was seduced by the harmony of the buildings and the small-scale, gentle charm of the surrounding countryside. I explored the Limpley Stoke valley in a trance and had an irrational sense of being bewitched. There certainly is a contrast between this enchanted world and the conventional sort of northern landscape that millions of us glimpse in miniature every year while crossing the Pennines on the M62. Yet glance to the left as the motorway curves down into Lancashire, just before the blue overhead signs to that very northern-sounding town Milnrow, and you see a particularly graceful church spire. There is something amiss about it, rising like a needle from the broad shoulder of the Pennines. What makes it somehow softer and more delicate than the scattering of farmhouses and the odd terrace which are the only other buildings in the view? Why does it seem out of place?

Great Gable and Wastwater in the Lake District

I wondered that for years but the motorway held me in its thrall, with that need to keep going, to press on to Manchester, Liverpool or Preston. But the time came when I forced myself off on to the A663, turned left and left again and discovered that St Thomas' church, in Newhey, near Milnrow, although built of local sandstone which has blackened, has a spire of Bath stone. It was the conceit of two brothers, Benjamin and James Heap, who built the church in 1875 in memory of their father, a millowner in the town. Like the Crossleys, Akroyds and other wealthy but good-hearted business people, their family was one that stayed locally. Benjamin played the harmonium at Sunday school and his parents are still in the church, buried below a plaque paid for by their employees. They holidayed in Somerset and liked it as much as I did. Hence St Thomas. It is a replica of Holy Trinity church in Weston-super-Mare.

Now it is one thing to import your own scenery like this, which few of us can afford to do. But that was never necessary. Return along

Britain's longest private home: Wentworth Woodhouse in Rotherham

the M62 eastwards to its very end, continue through Hull, and what a glorious vision rises like another slender needle from the flat land beyond Sunk Island! This is the 'Queen of Holderness', St Patrick's church in Patrington, whose limestone glows by day and looks almost translucent at night. So does the stonework on the nearby 'King of Holderness', St Augustine's in Hedon, and both resemble the transplanted church at Newhey in this regard. But neither of these is transplanted. Nor is the great limestone tower of Howden Minster which we passed on the motorway where it crosses the Ouse near its confluence with the Humber; great, but rising as lightly as the airships which they built at Howden until the crash of the Bedfordshire-built R101 in 1931 brought work to a halt. Nor is the delicate complex of gables and ogee-capped turrets at Ledston Hall, which shimmers out of a quiet valley between – astonishingly – Leeds and Castleford. Anyone not in the know shown a picture of this mansion and asked to guess its whereabouts would probably say the Cotswolds and would certainly never plump for Leeds. The hall was quarried from

a shining bed of magnesian limestone, which for all the dominance of millstone grit, gritstone and the other wutheringites, runs north through Ledston, Tadcaster and Boston Spa, from Cresswell Crags near Worksop where Britain's oldest artworks, cave paintings made 13,000 years ago, were discovered in 2003. It also passes through Conisbrough, seat of the celebrated 12th-century castle which is another glowing monument like Ledston Hall. It overlooks a valley of which Sir Walter Scott says in *Ivanhoe*: 'There are few more beautiful or striking scenes in England.' More prosaically I would say the same about the A630 from Doncaster to Rotherham, through places such as Conisbrough and Hooton Roberts.

The north-west too, despite the concentration of red brick in Manchester, Liverpool and Preston, has its share of limestone, especially on the tranquil plateau between the M6 summit at Shap and the towns along the river Lune. In Eden, that wide and well-named valley, the houses – and castles – are built in the local, warm red stone which reappears the other side of the Lake District and gives charm to Workington, as well as Muncaster and St Bees. As for scenery, there are the army ranges at Warcop where the absence of people encourages marvellous wildlife, including badgers who use the ground pounded up by the heavy guns firing into the fellside to construct what are probably England's deepest setts. The new forest planted by the Ministry of Defence on its other huge exercise area around Otterburn in Northumberland has 200,000 broadleaf trees which shelter wildlife and plants as well as soldiers on patrol. Ponds dug as ambush obstacles amid the trees double as homes for frogs, newts and toads which were very much scarcer before, and thick scrub conceals not only field headquarters but foxes and deer.

I will not labour the point, except to include the industrial north-east where the legacy of mining and predominance of dark-coloured sandstone does not mean that entirely different landscapes cannot be found too. To believe that would be to suppress Swinburne, that lyrical poet who exclaimed with delight every time he was invited by the Trevelyan family to Wallington Hall. 'That bright household in our joyous north,' he called it, while surrounding Northumberland was 'The crowning county in England – yes, the best!' Shortly before writing this, I was listening to a radio report on the Tees estuary as the supposed 'toxic waste dumping ground' of Britain. Perhaps it is, but look at the panorama they have in Middlesbrough and Billingham of the Cleveland escarpment and the north's own version of the Matterhorn, Roseberry Topping. We must paint the north in light as well as dark, as the writer Winifred Holtby did in 1937 in her *Letters to A Friend* where she pines for 'the light spray of larches, like green fountains springing among the warm darkness of firs.' The image is immediate for all who know the woodlands of the north.

But I am jumping ahead of myself. The areas I have described are the north's grandest green landscape, and I want to start lower down, on the doorstep which provided me as a boy with Elephant Hawk-Moth caterpillars and Great Crested Newts. Reach the western end of the M62 at Liverpool and what sign do you see, next to the one to the suburb of Knotty Ash, made famous by Ken Dodd? One which directs you to the National Wildflower Centre, a £4m Lottery project which is based less than a mile away in Court Hey Park. Come into Manchester town hall and cross the bees, the rectangle of floorspace at the top of the main staircase on the first floor where the otherwise uniform tile pattern of cotton flowers is replaced by that other symbol of the city, the industrious bee. This is reserved traditionally for city councillors to meet and exchange a private word – 'on the bees' is a euphemism for a confidential exchange. That is not our business, however. Beyond the bees is the great hall where grand civic events take place and on the walls of this are enormous Victorian paintings by Ford Madox Brown showing heroic scenes from Manchester's past.

Castle Howard mausoleum. A northern Arcadia

The one that always detains me shows John Dalton the chemist discovering marsh fire gas in a local pond, with the city sketched in dimly in the distance and wildflowers filling the foreground. He is surrounded and watched by rosy urchins, who were probably placing bets as to whether his precarious spectacles would topple into the water if he stretched out too far from the bank with his collecting bottles. It requires concentration to remember that this episode led to Dalton's atomic theory.

The painting encapsulates the mixture of town and country, grime and grass, which is so characteristic of the urban north. It is not unique to the region; I have spent many happy hours exploring London bombsites and railway land, whose willowherb and buddleia are rich hunting grounds for a moth and butterfly enthusiast. *The World My Wilderness* by Rose Macaulay gives their flavour perfectly. But there is an exceptional amount up here because so much countryside was replaced by houses and factories during and after the Industrial Revolution. The collieries of Conisbrough and Denaby were built in that valley which entranced Sir Walter Scott. Charles Reade sets his 1891 novel *Put Yourself in His Place* in what he calls 'perhaps the most hideous town in all creation' – Sheffield – but adds crucially and in an echo of Scott that the hideousness had been built on 'one of the loveliest sites in England.' Today, the hideousness is in full retreat, and the loveliness is back, and linked to the wider green world beyond the city limits. You reach the countryside far more quickly from Sheffield, Manchester, Newcastle, Leeds and Liverpool than anyone can from the enormous mass of London. The cities' green wedges and corridors also reach further in.

Soon after I moved from Bath to work in Bradford, a notice went up outside a Methodist chapel announcing a welcome service for 'Our new minister, who has come to us from Ryde on the Isle of

Wight.' I briefly had a strong fellow feeling and wondered about seeking him out to commiserate. But within a few days, I realised that the hills surrounding Bradford have exactly the same effect as those that hold Bath in its bowl. The view from Bath to Claverton Down was echoed by the green sweep of Queensbury one way, Thornton another and Undercliffe a third. Claverton's Sham Castle folly even had its equivalent in the soaring obelisk to Joseph Smith, the land agent who laid out Undercliffe's wonderful Victorian cemetery, with his contract reserving the best and most prominent plot in the place to take in due course his own remains.

In neighbouring Leeds, it is possible to deceive yourself that you are still in the countryside on three different approaches by foot, until you are less than half-a-mile from the town hall. The Leeds & Liverpool canal plays the trick most successfully, with a lovely sweep of greenery, including two fine willow trees, following the curve of the river Aire right up to the central railway station, where the water tumbles into the the vaults beneath the platforms and tracks, known as the Dark Arches. The Meanwood valley winds through the landscaped romantic wilderness of the Hollies park, crosses Meanwoodside where radical businessmen laid out an American garden in the 1790s to honour George Washington's rebels, and then enters a broad valley of fields on one side and the allotments and woods of the Ridge on the other. It is extraordinarily broad, so near to the tower blocks of Little London, and yet bucolic. The fields surround the Meanwood valley urban farm with its turf roof and provide grazing for its sheep and cattle. In the beck, you can not only paddle but if you are lucky, dig out civil war bullets from the battle of Woodhouse Ridge in 1643 which is part of this valley's rich history.

The third green wedge slopes gently down from the mossy foundations of the old isolation hospital at Killingbeck, a hillside

Green corridor. The Leeds and Liverpool canal in Lancashire

ridged by the traces of prehistoric earthworks, either defensive or agricultural. At the bottom is another stream, the Wyke Beck, which Keith Waterhouse tried to navigate as a boy in a raft he called the *Spirit of Leodis*, combining Leeds' Roman name with memories of Charles Lindbergh's Atlantic crossing aircraft. He was not an enthusiast for the wide green spaces of the new Halton Moor corporation estate where his family had been rehoused. The aim of his voyage was to get back to the relentlessly urban but cosy rows of red-brick terraces in Hunslet where he was born. Had he done so 150 years earlier, he would have grounded at Sandy Lobby, Leeds' very own beach on the river Aire. The Victorian journalist Tom Bradley described how in the 1790s the Lobby was 'a place where sportive lads bathed joyously on hot summer evenings in the clear water.' I have no doubt that before I retire, they will again. The Manchester rock group Stone Roses claim that their city 'has got everything except a beach,' but this will not be lacking for long in Leeds. Salmon, otters and kingfishers are already back in the city centre, as is another of Bradley's vignettes from the past: 'The stalwart youth would also take his manly exercise in the swift-gliding boats that were sent merrily o'er the Aire's surface, or in the evening would row some town-bred damsel of his choice over pleasant lengths of the stream.' Today, you can get a strawberries and cream cruise up towards Kirkstall Abbey, and Bradford rowing club races its eights along the river between Bingley and Saltaire.

Boys splashing in rivers are iconic in northern imagery at Appleby-in-Westmorland during the horse fair in June. They cling to bridles or ride bareback as the animals are washed, neck-deep, in the river Eden. But there is a link here with Bradford too. Many of these animals add another rural touch to the city, which is on the horse-trading route between London, Appleby and Ireland. There can be few cities with so many horses pastured on any bit of greenery available. I once saw four of them, escapees, thunder up the Manchester Road dual carriageway followed, like OJ Simpson in Los Angeles, by a line of police cars. For the same feature on the subject, I interviewed Terry Singh, the amicable chief dog warden for Bradford at the time, although he should have been renamed chief cowboy because he sorted out 300 horses a year. 'I've just had Paul Stokes – a well-known traveller and horsedealer – at our pound, trying to barter down the £160 fee for collecting two horses which he'd tethered behind the derelict Dudley Hill Labour club,' he told me. 'He says he's got 40 more coming over on the boat from Ireland. So I says: Well, don't bring them here unless you've got somewhere to put them.'

Fig trees grow beside the Don below the M1 viaduct at Tinsley, germinated from snap tin, or lunchbox, leftovers flung by 19th century steelworkers into the river, which was warmer in those days because of factory effluent. They have their counterparts along the Aire through Armley in Leeds. This doorstep greenery of the northern cities is also partly the result of oversight, lost deeds or occasionally a landowner determined to preserve a patch of green. It is helped in many ways by the roller-coaster terrain. For years, I drove around our neighbouring Leeds suburb of Yeadon by car, because of time and busy-ness, calling at the supermarket, picking up undelivered post at the Royal Mail depot, filling up at a garage on the A65 and dropping off rubbish at the council's recycling dump. None of these are pretty places, but I discovered only in 2008 that they are linked by a lovely green corridor made by local volunteers and the council out of a former railway line and engine sheds. It forms a narrow, twisting valley complete with a tumbling stream and quiet ponds, all of it ablaze between April and September with wild flowers. Returning home, I checked it out on Google maps and started moving the cursor across Leeds to look for other telltale patches or strips of green. I can see this becoming a retirement hobby.

In a similar man-made way, greenery has returned thanks to sensible dentistry by planners, for example in the demolition of every other row of back-to-backs in Armley, the west Leeds hillside where Alan Bennett and Barbara Taylor Bradford were children at the same primary school a couple of years apart. Protests at the loss of small but sound housing, and all the Bennetty nostalgia that went with it, died away when the effect of opening space between the cramped parallel terraces became clear. My, it was green! Bin yards in Burley, closer to the city centre, have had the same effect on a smaller scale. The front walls which enclosed these house-sized intervals in back-to-back terraces were demolished and residents were encouraged to paint and plant in them, around the wheelie bins. One is themed like a Spanish beach; another crops excellent tomatoes every year. Vik Banks, who runs the fair trade clothing shop Akadash in Manchester but lives in Leeds, has taken the improvement one storey up, by obtaining the

Seabirds in Grimsby docks

city council's first grant to sow a living roof – selected grasses and hardy plants – above her kitchen extension. She got the knowhow from a Sheffield University stall at a green fair in Sheffield.

Wildlife prospers everywhere. When I was in Grimsby docks one January, enjoying the ragamuffin landscape of grotty buildings and patches of weedy wasteland, I counted 10 species of gull and wader and watched cormorants beating all of them to the fish. The *Manchester Guardian's* country diarist Arnold Boyd had exactly this experience in Birkenhead docks, when military duties in 1940 took him away from his usual, sweetly rural Cheshire patch near Knutsford, the town immortalised by Mrs Gaskell as Cranford, all rambling rose and bluebell wood. Initially glum at his urban surroundings, he was soon finding yellow wagtails in profusion on wasteground near the Seacombe ferry. There were meadow pipits there too, and a pair of skylarks. A week later he was starting his Country Diary: 'There is a flower garden in dockland…' and what a garden it proved to be.

Melilot, toadflax, tansy, sickle medick, greater knapweed, trefoils and dyer's mignonette; the last whose name is an exemplar of the north's *rus in urbe*, beautiful but also useful and growing handily for the textile mills. Ditto the millwort.

There is a painting in Bradford art gallery at Cartwright Hall which encapsulates this combination, an enormous canvas painted by Bertram Priestman in 1916 and called *The Heart of the West Riding*. Its great virtue is that it shows the predictable smoking chimneys, multi-storeyed mills and railway trains trundling about laden with goods, but that is only the half of it. Fields and gardens interrupt the buildings everywhere, as they still do. A fine stand of oak trees dominates one corner of the picture and in the background rise the Pennine hills, which remind so many towns and cities in the north that indisputable beauty is not far away. I have always wanted to build a layby on the M62 at Ainley Top, with a few picnic tables such as the French have where the A61 swoops past Carcassonne. They call them

Wildflowers at Runshaw near Wigan, Lancashire

aires over there, meaning eyrie, and from the one I propose, the view over the Calder valley from Elland, with Joe Kagan's Gannex mill in the foreground, makes my point with unforgettable style. This is the Bradford painting on an even larger canvas: a patchwork of beautiful countryside and towns which are lovely for a different reason: they offer jobs, homes and all the necessities for making a living.

You see the same in the north-east, tonning up the A1M past the Penshaw monument – fields and woods and in the distance Nissan with its wind turbines and factory roads named Cherry Tree Drive and the like, another nice mix of greenery and graft. You don't see it in many other parts of the north because of ribbon development. If you want to discover superlative nooks in Lancashire such as Crank or Pimbo, where I spent a drowsy summer afternoon with one of Britain's leading beekeepers, you've got to have the strength of mind to turn off the East Lancs road. The same applies on the A68 slanting SE to NW across County Durham, a scenic switchback through an area often stereotyped as one former pit village after another. In South Yorkshire I would build another *aire* on the M1 just south of the Barnsley turnoff, next to Arthur Scargill's house. Are those deer in the field across the road? They are. This is the Wentworth Castle estate where I successfully entranced my London mother-in-law with its prettiness. We went in late May and picnicked in a dell which was frothing with the whites, creams, lemons and pinks of the finest rhododendron collection in England. So fine, that when the Chinese government wanted to reintroduce a number of native rhododendrons that had become extinct in their country, they came to Wentworth for plants. To Barnsley? It's as dubious as the notion that a half-French Barnsley girl could write best-selling books about wild young women selling chocolate in Burgundy. As we have seen, Joanne Harris has rooted here as successfully as the rhododendrons.

She was not the first, by any means. There was Barry Hines' story *Kes*, about the misfit boy from Barnsley and the hawk he tames. The film version was a huge success in 1969 and the countryside was integral to that; not only did the boy find solace and his kestrel in the woods round the ruins of Tankersley Old Hall (which you also glimpse from the M1, a few miles south of Wentworth on the other side of the carriageways); but the beauty was so unexpected to so many cinema audiences. Did young Billy Casper's absolutely predictable red-brick council estate and entirely just-as-you'd-imagine-it comprehensive really give way, almost immediately, to such ravishing surroundings? The film needed sub-titles in America to cope with the broad South Yorkshire accents, all theeing and sen-ing. The countryside shots spoke for themselves.

Behind us as we gaze at Wentworth Castle, on the other side of the pretty Stainborough valley, is Hound Hill, an even older house and one of the homes of the Elmhirst family who helped to found Dartington Hall school down in Devon; more on them in due course. Goodness, you can see the top of Barnsley town hall from here, but how soft and gentle is everything else! And we haven't even started yet. Barnsley has 127 square miles of open countryside, some of it in the five-star landscape of the Peak District national park.

The greenery of northern towns and their immediate neighbour-hoods such as Stainborough is only a preface to that much grander countryside signalled by the Pennine view. For all their concentration on slum life and the hard grind of mill work, memoirs and novels of life in the urban north almost always have a sense that the countryside is very near: freedom and fresh air just a bus ride or even walk from those donkey-stoned front steps. Howard Spring makes this fundamental to the character of Harmer Shawcross, the hero of *Fame is the Spur*, a Mancunian working in Bradford whose visions of

Northern townscape; a hotchpotch of green and grey

socialism and a redeemed humanity are at their most intense as he
strides from Dick Hudson's famous walkers' pub on to Ilkley Moor.
Composing the novel in 1938-9, Spring was certainly writing with
Priestley's *English Journey* in mind, a book published only six years
earlier which describes Bradford accurately as 'hardly more than a
tram-ride away from wild Pennine country. A man might spend his
mornings on the Wool Exchange and then spend his evenings among
moorland folk who would not do badly as characters in the medieval
Wakefield Nativity Play.' Wuthering Heights are only just round the
corner.

And talking of them: the aptly-named Brontë industry has
invested a lot in pretending that the landscape stretching for wide,
empty miles round Haworth is brooding, dour and probably
rainswept, the very essence of northern cliché. That is not how the
sisters saw it. Charlotte wrote of Emily: 'My sister loved the moors.
Flowers brighter than the rose bloomed in the blackest of the heath
for her; out of a sullen hollow in a livid hillside her mind could
make an Eden. She found in the bleak solitude many and dear
delights.' Emily herself has Cathy Earnshaw daydreaming about 'a
hot July day lying from morning to evening on a bank of heather
with the bees humming dreamily amid the bloom, the larks singing
and the blue sky and bright sun shining steadily overhead. She
wanted to be clambering in a green tree with not just the larks but
the blackbirds, thrushes and linnets, and wanting all to sparkle
and dance.' When Charlotte worked as a governess at Upwood in
Rawdon, half a mile from where I am writing this and in the heart
of the West Riding mill district, she noted in her diary: 'The place
looks exquisitely beautiful just now – the grounds are lovely and
green as an emerald.' They still are. I can be there in 10 minutes on
foot from my front door.

Priestley's description is just as true now as it was then, apart from the Wool Exchange being a Waterstone's branch and the trams buses. It is also typically northern, in that you genuinely travel very swiftly from busy city to countryside as untamed and grand as any seeker of the Sublime could wish. The speed of the transition has attracted many would-be incomers, including the Queen who has twice let slip that if she were ever to retire, her first choice of retreat would be the Trough of Bowland in Lancashire. Leaks about this prompted many northern memories of the Princess Royal, sister of King George VI, who married the Earl of Harewood, moved to Leeds and was photographed annually by the *Yorkshire Post*, pruning her rose garden at Harewood House. Unfortunately for the north, the Queen does not seem to be the retiring kind.

It would be redundant to spend part of a chapter redescribing the wonders that attract her, and millions of other visitors annually, to the gold-star northern wilds, including the five national parks. Whole libraries have been written about them, with immortal names on many of the book spines, and they are now supplemented by hours of TV and film. Better, to look at how and why these immortals were transfixed by their surroundings and – given the number of describers which is almost as spectacular as the landscape itself – to choose two different ones to make the point.

Wordsworth first; he stands out for me from the lustrous ranks of the other Lakes poets through the power of *The Prelude*. When I visit the Wordsworth house in Cockermouth, I can imagine it all in terms of my own fortunate boyhood. My soul had fair seed time too. It was therefore comparatively easy to travel on with him to the state of almost-ecstasy induced by the glories of the Lakes. When I first read the poem I was at an old wooden desk in Shrewsbury School. When I first felt it, I was a teenager walking alone from Helm Cragg round

Strolling by the Wear in Sunderland, 1976

by Greenup Edge to Sergeant Man and back down Silver Howe on a baking hot, blue-sky day in July when I felt you could love the landscape physically. Was this the monopoly of privilege and an expensive education? No. Because my second exemplar came from a completely different background.

He shared only his surname with me. Otherwise, Alfred Wainwright the celebrated fellwalker, writer and mapmaker, came from the opposite sort of childhood and background: a drunken failure for a father, no money to spare in a backstreet, Blackburn terrace-house upbringing and a family imprisoned by social constraints which led him to make a disastrous first marriage. But he stood beside Wordsworth when he scrambled up Orrest Head for the first time, in 1930 at the age of 23 on his first real holiday from clerical work in the borough engineer's office at Blackburn. Lakeland lay before him, as though a curtain had been torn aside, as much from his own eyes as in the mist which so often hides the tops. He was transfixed and enthralled to find that landscapes which he had only imagined previously were true and real. Those two concepts had always been confined to what in his world had been routinely called 'the real world': nine-to-five work and narrow horizons in Blackburn.

So anyone can benefit. You don't have to be naturally cheerful or comfortably positioned. You don't even have to be physically in the hills or by the lakes, so long as you have been, once upon a time. A special spot for me is a modest plaque overlooking St Nicholas churchyard at Amen Corner in Newcastle upon Tyne. I chanced on it one chilly January day after I had clambered up Dog Bank from a job at the courthouse on the Quayside and was threading my way through underpasses and alleys to the railway station. As I packed up my computer in the lobby outside the courtroom, the sunset was just beginning to cast a warm light along the Tyne, reflected by the striking curves of the Sage in Gateshead and illuminating the winking bridge. When I got outside, very quietly the fog was rolling up the Tyne from the sea, engulfing the High Level bridge as I watched until only a fragment of girder and curve could be made out. As I marched upwards, the fog came with me and soon everything seemed deserted and still. I hurried on in the twilight, wondering if single footsteps were following me or whether the shadow in a doorway was a lurker. But when I saw the plaque I stopped. It was topped by a neatly-sculpted bust of Thomas Bewick and said that this was his workshop. Everything in sight was brick or stone, and most of it would have been in his day in the 18th and early 19th centuries. But what visions of the countryside were engraved inside this building, by a man who knew that they were very close at hand.

I am a serial hymn-singer when alone in the car, and the simple phrase 'close at hand' reminds me of *Wise Men Seeking Jesus* which, like Bewick's engravings, conjures up exactly this sense of beautiful nearby greenery in the heads of people working in northern towns. Its origins make the same point. The writer James Thomas East was a Manchester man who saved up to visit the Holy Land in the early years of the 20th century, but then spent his money instead on medical treatment for a friend who was seriously ill in those pre-NHS days. His hymn was written to pass on the revelation brought by this experience: that there is no need to go to the Middle East to experience the meaning of Bethlehem because:

> ...*if we desire Him*
> *He is close at hand*
> *For our native country*
> *Is our Holy Land.*

Leaving aside theology, the seven verses are full of references to quiet lakes, hillsides at dawn and fishermen beside the North Sea which were as real to East in his Manchester home as when he was out enjoying them. Bewick likewise, and do not succumb to any feeling that his delicate art was in contrast to 'rugged' or 'wild' surroundings. The countryside he roamed on Tyneside and Wearside is among the driest places in Britain and warmer on average in January than inland East Anglia and the Thames valley. Lady Elizabeth Montagu was way off beam (but of course got all the headlines and later literary references) when she affected to believe in the 1750s that Newcastle lay beyond the Arctic Circle. She didn't really believe it, of course. She was born Elizabeth Robinson, daughter of a Yorkshire squire at West Layton, now just off the A66 near Scotch Corner, the beginning of the last lap from the south to the Tyne. But many of those who have subsequently quoted her with a genteel shudder at the obstacles she braved on her northern travels overlooked her skill at irony.

Geltsdale grouse moor, Cumbria, run by the RSPB

Bewick thoroughly enjoyed Newcastle and would surely be pleased to know that in 2009, 181 years after his death, the busy city has more flower shops per head of population than anywhere else in England. After giving London a try and returning home within the year, he wrote: 'I would rather live in both poverty and insecurity in Newcastle. All the numerous shows to be seen in London may give a momentary satisfaction but cannot afford me half the pleasure which I always felt in my excursions through the quiet woods to Eltringham.'

His spirit, and that of Thomas East, also inform the Lancashire Friends of Walt Whitman, who have held Whitman Days since 1885 on the birthday of the great American laureate of the countryside. Fortunately this falls on May 31, when the beauties of the north are at their best, and a scroll through past Whitman Day venues is a rollcall of Lancashire's loveliest places. To take just one, in 1913 the disciples went to pretty little Rivington, under Rivington Pike only eight miles from Bolton, to picnic and read the master's works. Their base, reported the *Annandale Observer* newspaper, was in the parsonage grounds of the quiet old Unitarian chapel – 'the unsophisticated charm of which can nowhere be surpassed.' Nowhere, note. Nowhere in the whole world.

I was lucky to learn the same lesson over a cup of tea with Harry Griffin, the *Guardian* country diary writer, at his Kendal flat. In his 90s, he was no longer able to climb Napes Needle or even walk as far as Wainwright's Orrest Head above Windermere, but he described them as precisely and lovingly as he had in the course of his record-breaking 53 years on the column. "Do you think I'm boring the readers by going on about these places, because I can't get out so much?" he would ask. No one was bored.

This would be an exultant moment to end this chapter, but there are two further, important points to make, the first one partly contradictory of the weight I have given to wildness and the abundance, within easy reach, of unspoiled natural beauty. Although the Sublime scenery of the region is enormous and epic, it is seldom as untrodden as it appears. A careless walker on Coniston Old Man or Wetherlam can come to grief in dozens of vertically-sided quarries or collapsed copper mine tunnels; indeed Wainwright, trapped in his miserable marriage, gloomily suggested that they might be places to dispose of unwanted wives. Graphite made fortunes in Borrowdale, a mineral so rare and valuable for military use as well as pencil leads that Royal troops were sent from London to guard shipments out of the valley. Other precious veins did the same for alum manufacturers on the North Yorkshire coast, once knowledge of the smelting process had been smuggled out of the Vatican. In fairness to the south, London urine shipped north as ballast for returning coal ships from Newcastle was another essential part of the process.

Harry Griffin in his beloved Lake District

Even the precipitous sea cliffs at Bempton on the North Sea coast between Flamborough and Filey were work-providers and money-earners. Until 1954, farmers and fishermen earned extra cash by dangling over the edge to winkle eggs out of seabirds' nests in the crannics, some to eat, others to go into the process of dressing patent leather and a few, from the rarer species, to sell at high prices to naturalists and birds' egg collectors. They hammered their iron stakes, to belay their ropes, into fields which in recent years have added vivid colours to the local landscape via another ingenious business: the mass cultivation of 'everlasting flowers' for interior decorators and other brightly-petalled species for 'natural' confetti. In true northern style, the egg-collecting industry also fostered a spin-off trade through the hand-knitted fishermen's ganseys for the 'climmers' to protect them from both foul weather and the sharp ledges of the cliffs. An even more remote example of work in the wilderness was discovered by Harry Griffin at the top of Bowfell buttress in the Lake District, above 2,500ft and on the edge of the highest plateau in England: a shepherd's tiny storm refuge which just houses a grown man, if you snuggle in bottom first. And if you think the unusual Alpines growing in the cliff above the lake behind Ingleborough Hall got there naturally, think again. Their seeds were collected overseas by the celebrated plantsman Reginald Farrer whose family still owns the estate, and fired into the unreachable crevices by his shotgun to see if they would take in England.

This 'usefulness' of even the most inaccessible parts of the northern countryside is not just a matter of history. One of the comforts of negotiating the difficult crossing from Black Sail to Borrowdale in Cumbria when the mist swirls down, is the nearby clang and clunk of slate-cutting machines working for the flourishing Honister Pass mine. It may seem a little demeaning for a proud walker navigating the coast-to-coast path which traverses the featureless top of this bowl, but humbly asking an excavator-driver where you are is preferable to walking round in circles, damp and cold.

The exploitation of these lovely spots has also often been on an enormous and environmentally disastrous scale. The climmers may be quaint, but the lead-miners who used 'hushing' – the release of dammed water to sweep the entire top and subsoil strata off underlying lead seams – turned the hilltops north of Swaledale into something resembling the moon. After they left, stonecrushers moved in to turn the rubble into aggregate for road foundations, but the landscape created by these two devastating heavy industries now has a wilderness atmosphere of its own, and is deservedly part of the Yorkshire Dales national park. Heather and bilberries are very slowly creeping back in, and starlets of yellow tormentil line the paths down to ruined smelting mills, which have the heroic atmosphere of small Norman castles, or miniature secular versions of the Yorkshire abbeys.

The coppery coloured beck below Buzzard Scar attracts herb robert, maidenhair fern and New Zealand willowherb where it tumbles past Swinner Gill Kirk, a cave used for services by both Catholic and Nonconformist dissidents to escape the regulations of the established church in troubled times.

Small wonder that many walkers resting at Crackpot Hall, the former deerkeeper's lodge where the paths down the dale divide, chose the mines and moors rather than the more conventionally beautiful riverside walk along the Swale. Certainly, they would have been the choice of WH Auden. Born in York, and often taken on holidays as a child to Appletreewick in Wharfedale, a place as pretty as its name, he joined Wordsworth, Wainwright and all the others as a man moulded by these surroundings. He developed a particular interest in lead-mining after visiting such places as Kirkhope in upper Teesdale, a place where you can enjoyably make children's blood run

Wainwright's favourite: Innominate Tarn on Haystacks

Climbing Helvellyn towards Striding Edge

cold. Water pours eternally from the mine tunnel entrance. Beyond, in the darkness, a huge waterwheel pumps it up from lower levels where miners would otherwise have drowned. The inexorable turning of the wheel in the gloom is frightening enough, but what of the day when horrified workers in the yard below the mine saw the water suddenly turn red? Two men had been caught by the wheel which cannot be stopped instantly – it would crush any spanner flung in to jam its works.

Auden was fascinated by lead-mining country and by the geology below it, especially the limestone whose vulnerability to erosion and the steady drip-drip of hidden water is so at odds with the vast and permanent air of the hills. Like lead, the stone is soft and he used this paradox in his verse, particularly the poem 'In Praise of Limestone' which he wrote in 1948 when his exile from Britain became permanent. Inconstant by nature, he wrote, men and women were especially homesick for the proud and beautiful rock with its hidden weakness.

...when I try to imagine a faultless love
Or the life to come, what I hear is the murmur
Of underground streams, what I see is a limestone
  landscape.

Thus the poem ends, after adding this last but crucial clue to the essence of the green north. Northerners know it, consciously or simply as part of our upbringing – the way that we learned to explore these landscapes rather than receiving them in the post as Christmas calendars which you can't climb into, Narnia-like, when they hang on the wall. In my own case, the contrast was especially striking because it involved Ilkley Moor, which in the cliché depends on foul weather, bleak surroundings and blunt characters. My Ilkley Moor is none of those. Take the little switchback road from Menston to the Cow and Calf rocks via Burley Woodhead and, just beyond a turreted mansion and a garden centre, strike off uphill through the bracken by a tumbling stream. There are miniature meadows, the size of a picnic rug, and a little higher up the narrow clough which eventually leads to the moortop, small-scale waterfalls sheltered by rowan trees. This is Robin Hole, equal favourite picnic place for us as children with the lost world of Lindley mill race in the Washburn valley (now, alas, a fish farm). Go in July, take tomatoes and a pie, curl up on the rug and enjoy unashamedly the warm sun. It's sweet and pretty, soft and lovely, but very much part of the north.

6

The Gift of Newcomers

'This was my world, and I was not unhappy with it...
Leeds was my city, and I slowly developed a great
pride in it.'
Caryl Phillips, revisiting his childhood home
for the *Guardian* in 2005

If you Google 'the north' and 'immigration' and click the UK only button, you might think it perverse of me to hold up new arrivals in our region, from penniless Russian Jews to Kashmiris without a word of English, as one of the great attractions of living here. But it is so. Book-burning, riots, palava about wearing burkas at Jack Straw's surgery in Blackburn? Yes, they have all happened, but they are the froth and not the substance of the vital transfusion that re-energises the north with new blood. The substance is fresh ideas from hard-working, eager, clever people who want to get stuck in. We need lots of them. People who want to be British and even better, northern, but not on entirely one-sided terms. Great! What better than to add yet more ingredients to our already enormous and complex mix? Who wants to live in a monochrome world – or delude themselves that such a thing is possible anyway?

It was certainly never that way in my childhood, even in a north Leeds suburb that superficially might have appeared to be overwhelmingly white. We had regular visitors from all over the world via the university, church, chapel and family, including a genial Ghanaian who widened our horizons by staying for Christmas and dressing up as Santa (when we still believed in him coming down the chimney and eating the rock buns we left out). When we leafed through the pages of out-of-date *Leeds Tatlers* at the dentist, we always encountered Lady Bomanji, a leading figure in local society and good works during the 1950s. Pestering my parents about Titty, the odd name of one of the young heroes of *Swallows and Amazons*, I discovered that it came from a real-life fellow northern child with an even more unusual name – Altounyan – whose father had emigrated from Armenia to Manchester to work as a doctor. Betty's café, where we occasionally went for treats, was founded by a Swiss immigrant, Frederick Belmont, and our ice creams in Scarborough were made by an Italian, Peter Jaconelli. Another Italian dynasty founded by an itinerant pedlar, the Fattorinis, owned Skipton Castle and, more importantly, made our badges saying 'Jo Grimond, Liberal leader.' Most exotic of all was the story of the Japanese chicken-sexers who were taken to heart by the clannish Pennine village of Cowling, near Skipton. Messrs Goshide, Hattori and Tanigushir could sort chicks at an extraordinary 1,200 an hour. Although they had to go back to Japan in 1939 and two were killed during the war, the survivor returned for a visit in his retirement and was given a fond welcome.

These people were part of our community, but what about us, the ones whose ancestors had been here for centuries? There was plenty of mixture in our little bodies too. One of the most salutary news stories I have written concerned a proposal for voluntary genetic

Moss Side, Manchester, in the summer of 1957

tests on people living at the Cumbrian end of Hadrian's Wall, where legionaries recruited from north African provinces of the empire served at the fort of Aballava, where Burgh by Sands now looks out over the Solway Firth. Soldiers seldom leave the local women alone and geneticists were sure that they would find traces of black ancestry. They did.

A similar mix in a slightly different form is described by the historian Christopher Grocock at the other end of the wall. He pictures the seventh and eighth century monk the Venerable Bede leaving his monastery in Jarrow for a walk into town, where he would have heard a rich mixture of Latin, Old English and Celtic, perhaps with a smattering of Norse in the melting pot too. The link to the 21st century is direct. Grocock compares Bede's world to his own shopping calls at a newsagent's in Jarrow where he is served by two women who speak to him in English, with a Geordie accent, in between chattering to one another in Urdu. Then as now, the liveliness and interest of a cosmopolitan world was balanced by tensions; Bede himself refers to monastery colleagues who had not mastered Latin as 'idiotae' because they knew only their cruder native tongues (although I remember from university that his own Latin wasn't exactly the one that poshers spoke in Rome).

None of the difficulties between northern communities of the last few decades is new, either. Every late 20th century slur on Pakistanis has its early 20th century equivalent about the Jews ('filthy, dirty, the lowest and worst sort') or the 19th century Irish, whose supposedly inbred slumminess led to typhus being nicknamed the Irish disease. Both of those groups, and other incomers before and since, reacted

Cultures meet in Burnley, 1977

to racism by rioting. In the Jewish and Irish cases that actually led to deaths, which have been almost entirely avoided in British civil disturbances since the second world war, other than those relating to Northern Ireland. Foreign policy complications, such as we have now with parts of the Muslim world, were familiar too. Britain was never unconnected with the countries from which immigrants had moved to better themselves, or simply fled. Today's strained loyalties for some Muslims would be recognisable to British Jews in the late 1940s, when British soldiers were being killed in Palestine, including the hanging of three captured sergeants which matched in cold-hearted brutality the video-murders posted by al-Qaida.

The experience of Jewish immigrants to the north is well-documented, in the way that current community relations certainly will be thanks to the proliferation of the media. This is hardly surprising from a community which has produced so many talented people, and it throws up parallel after parallel. Young Jews attended Hebrew classes just like the children in white and green who throng to the mosque madrasas in modern Bradford. The youth organisation of Zionism, the Habonim, marched in uniform through the streets in the 1920s and 30s, like the scouts, guides and boys and girls brigades. There were annual Palestine bazaars in Leeds and Manchester and few Jewish homes were without a collecting box for the Jewish national fund.

More potentially troublesome, until Britain and Zionism came into direct conflict after the second world war, was the Jewish community's association with communism. In Leeds, half the party's members in the late 1930s were Jewish as were a quarter of those who went to fight against Franco in Spain (not a direct comparison with going to Afghanistan, but there are ideological parallels). Older members of the community worked actively against this, as today's moderate mosque elders do with potentially radical young Islamists, and for the same reason: anti-semitism was feared in the same way as Islamophobia is now. There was every reason for them to do so. In 1920, the *Yorkshire Post* referred to irritation caused by the parade of flashily-dressed young Jews along the main shopping street of Leeds, Briggate. It deplored such prejudice, pointing out that every sort of teenager in the city could put on a swagger too. But the same paper's golf correspondent maintained that Jews and gentiles 'just don't mix' and, disgracefully, that was the case in the game until relatively recent times.

Swastika posters were plastered on Jewish-owned shops when Sir Oswald Mosley's blackshirts rallied on Holbeck Moor in September 1936 (over 30,000 people went, for and against). Innuendo about Jews turning council houses into shops was commonplace. In response, informally-organised groups of tough young Jews guarded synagogues and sometimes went further. The 101 Club, which advertised itself 'For English clientele only' – a euphemism for 'no Jews' – was broken into and trashed.

The Irish in the north faced exactly the same treatment, with exaggerated fears about their living conditions, numbers and alleged disloyalty. From the first, they had to put up with sneers such as that in the *Economic Journal* which visited Manchester in 1899 and put a hanky to its nose at conditions in the city's rag trade but added: 'Dirty as the work is, it would be affectation for the Irish to object to it very strongly on that ground.' Eighty years later, the staff at Leeds Irish Club described how they sat in the dark with the curtains closed, for fear of retaliation, on the night after the IRA murder of Lord Mountbatten in 1979. Sheffield's very-longstanding Yemeni community lay low in a similar way in 1967 when 18 British soldiers were killed in a single attack by insurgents in Aden.

Moss Side, Manchester, 1971

But none of this led to communal breakdown in the long term, nor even to a pause in the enormous contribution made by immigrant communities, especially economically. Thank goodness. Where would the north be today without the Irish and the Jews? How immensely much feebler our cities would be, had they not welcomed Armenians and Greeks in the chaos after the first world war, and Poles, Ukrainians and Balts after the second. West Indians, Pakistanis, Indians, Bangladeshis and most recently more Eastern Europeans are part of the same distinguished procession. Leeds University alone has students from 127 countries and every one is a reason to cheer. The cheers have an echo going back years. There would be no Leeds Caribbean Carnival, the second oldest and biggest in Britain after Notting Hill, without the work of the city's St Kitts and Nevisians. Exiled Czechs set up Fulneck school in Pudsey.

Chinese New Year celebrations in Manchester

Louis le Prince from Metz in France pioneered cinema in Leeds and took the world's first motion pictures in 1888 in Roundhay Park and beside Leeds Bridge.

There is also an interesting sidebar to the troublesome history of assimilation: the way that each immigrant group's experience helps the rest of us in the north to learn. Their dissent is a check on assumptions that the British way of doing things is best – for example that our foreign policy is as ethical as Robin Cook, Tony Blair's first foreign secretary, vainly hoped it might become. And when things get violent, that too is useful, as a reminder that the energy and anger itself is more British than many of us like to think. We have a national habit of forgetting that violence has preceded almost every worthwhile reform in our history, to challenging and – usually – ending injustice when the ballot and peaceful disobedience fail.

Even book burning? Yes, deplorable though it was, the *Satanic Verses* stunt in Bradford in 1988 was neither original nor some fanatical ritual imported from out east. In 1893, not 15 miles from Bradford, the Bishop of Wakefield not only publicly burnt Thomas Hardy's *Jude the Obscure* but made sure that the *Yorkshire Post* knew the time and place, and then managed to get the novel banned from all circulating libraries in his diocese. The parallels are exact. The Rushdie book-burning was moved forward by 20 minutes because my old colleague Derek Chapman of the *Bradford Telegraph & Argus* had another job to get to. Both were disastrous own goals. But the contrast between deeply hurt members of a minority religion doing such a stupid thing, and a deeply hypocritical pillar of the late Victorian establishment doing the same, is worth thinking about.

I wonder, too, if there is a particularly northern fellow-feeling with energetic protest. I covered both the virtually all-white Meadowell riots on Tyneside in 1991 and the largely British Asian ones in

Bradford 10 years later. Talking to participants in both, I was struck by the sense in which each group felt disadvantaged and on the periphery, and suddenly sensed a feeling of empowerment through briefly – very briefly - having some sort of upper hand. Extending the parallel, I asked young men in Bradford if they felt that tradition went back to their parents' roots overseas. Hardly any were from Pakistan's equivalents of London and the south, Karachi and the coast. Most were from the independent-minded 'edge', Kashmir and Mirpur, and, yes, they thought, it was pretty fanciful but maybe mum and dad had practice in being northerners over there. Another told a reporter up from London, with a grin and a clear command of Yorkshire word structure: 'We're dead contrary, us.' Both generations sensed the remoteness and lack of interest in their problems at the centre of power, which was explicitly described by Yasmin Alibhai-Brown who was a journalist on the *New Statesman* at the time of the *Satanic Verses* incident. She wrote in the *Independent* after the 2001 troubles in Bradford:

'I had tried in vain to persuade the editor to let me go to the city in the weeks before the book-burning, because I knew of the growing fury and hopelessness that had engulfed Muslims in Yorkshire. They felt Salman Rushdie had deliberately set out to insult their faith. The story was not of any interest I was told. For the metropolitan élite, excitable brown chaps who had read the Koran but not Proust were of no consequence. Then the book was burnt and Bradford made history.'

Subjects always interest you if you have a personal connection, and I was convinced that I had my own fellow-feeling with the rioters. In my family's case the peripheral incomers were long ago, probably Norse raiders whose initial treatment of the north – effectively suppressing Christianity on the Yorkshire coast for two

Women mourn a fatal house fire, Bradford 1980

centuries – didn't suggest that they would ever integrate and settle down. I was in my early twenties when I made my own landfall in Bradford and although I was born within 10 miles of the *Telegraph & Argus* office, I considered myself to be an immigrant and thought it prudent to behave cautiously. I was not arriving from the foothills of the Himalayas or the Caribbean's palm-lined shores, but from an equally foreign country called Bath, where I had worked for the local *Evening Chronicle* for three and a half years. Sheffield's *Morning Telegraph* offered me one job and the *T&A* another, which I went for because the city intrigued me while Sheffield at the time – 1975 – was associated with industrial decline. It was also the old enemy of my native Leeds; at school I had battled over statistics with a Sheffield boy, each of us hunting all the time for new data which would prove that one or the other was bigger, more prosperous or the birthplace of more winners of the Victoria Cross.

This rivalry applied to Bradford too, of course, and was part of my immigrant status. Nowhere, not even London and the south, is less desirable to a northerner than the town next door. On a large scale, think Manchester and Liverpool or Sunderland and Newcastle. On a smaller one, Bingley and Shipley have nothing complimentary to say about one another and I have already mentioned the scorn in my current home, Rawdon, when it comes to Yeadon, a mile higher up the hill. Leeds and Bradford naturally fall into this sort of relationship, but it is a little more complex because Leeds has become so much the dominant partner. Bradford's fear of being thought inferior was particularly strong at the time of my move, because it was losing the grandeur of the wool industry which had given it the edge over Leeds in global terms. As JB Priestley said in one of his many accurate observations about his native town: 'You used to meet

Textile revival on a small but profitable scale

men who did not look as if they had ever been anywhere further than York or Morecambe [Bradfordians' favourite holiday choice, where the *T&A* had an office in summer], but who actually knew every continental express.'

By contrast, Leeds was known only for Leeds United in distant lands, apart possibly from Mongolia. The very strong ties between Ulan Bator and Leeds universities have led to a regular and welcome assumption among students there that Leeds is the capital of Britain, rather than London. This was certainly true when I was a teenager and was told about it by a Mongolian student called Altanchimeg who was slowly translating the Bible into the economical vocabulary of her native language. The power of Google may have since changed things in London's favour. But Bradford had always had the edge in terms of international fame, and by 1975 that consolation was fading.

At the time of my move, the city's thin skin was also being pricked by the affair of the Wortley loop, for which any incomer from Leeds might easily be blamed. The loop was a curve of railway track which allowed trains from London to bypass Leeds and speed on through Pudsey and then down the steep hill to Bradford Exchange station. The city could thereby continue to claim a direct service to the capital, even if there were not many of them. After much argument, the loop was closed and although the reason was train company efficiency, Bradford put the blame on Leeds.

By the time I started work in the former Milligan & Forbes textile warehouse which housed the *T&A*, Bradford had a long record of accepting immigrants and, of course, profiting from them, as did the wider north. Milligan himself, who had made the money to build my then workplace, was one of a group of Scots who effectively took over the strategic direction of Bradford's wool industry in the mid-19th century and turned the city from a highly productive manufacturing centre to the world's entrepôt for wool, with deals by woolmen from all manner of countries done in the Wool Exchange, just as they are by financiers today in the stock exchanges of London, Tokyo and New York. The Scots were followed by German merchants, including the family of the composer Frederick Delius, and then eastern Europeans caught up in the chaotic aftermath of the second world war who were directed to work in certain cities as a condition of staying in the United Kingdom.

These nationalities settled, often in fairly tight communities, and built their own clubs and churches – today, a Christmas enthusiast can still celebrate for much of December and early January in Bradford at the long series of different festivals offered by local varieties of Lutheranism, Catholicism and Orthodoxy. These could make them suddenly visible, as also happened during Estonian singing festivals or the annual Captive Nations Week when the flags of Soviet satellites which have since won their independence flew all around the town hall. But most of the time, they passed unremarked because their accents carried no social connotations and they looked no different from everyone else. They were white.

So was I, and I had plenty of other advantages over an Asian or Afro-Caribbean newcomer. But I had one drawback which allowed me just a sense of identifying with new Commonwealth immigrants: I talked posh. Accent matters less in the north now, but it was a factor 30 years ago. It was an invitation to prejudice, born of long associations of such voices with ignorant outsiders at best, and with an exploitative 'them' at worst – the reaction revived in the affair of the talking Leeds bus stops described in Chapter 3. I have seen other poshers hurt and resentful as a result, but I was ready for the treatment, partly because of my experience of reverse prejudice, when

Terrace and mosque in Blackburn

Sikhs at a community meeting in Leeds

I had to speak 'Yorkshire' in the school bogs at the age of seven. I had also spent time in Northern Ireland where it was instructive to be treated as a 'Brit' instead of an individual. That wasn't the case with everyone, any more than racism is for a black northerner, but my accent was certainly linked with historic misdeeds done in Ireland centuries before I was born.

I trod carefully in Bradford, therefore, learning a little from my father's subtly changing vowel sounds when he spoke in his constituency (an almost unconscious facility which is another of Hiram Yorke's habits in *Shirley* – see page 126). I also tried to work out how to soften that edge of assurance and implied (if unintended) superiority which can go with received pronunciation and make it offensive. In that, I was buoyed up by colleagues' friendliness; there was Dudley Akeroyd, the *T&A's* religious and military correspondent who sat opposite me when not in Belize or Cyprus on visits financed by the army to see Bradford squaddies doing their duty; there was

Pat McGowan, the crime man whose Saab packed with electronic gizmos intercepted emergency calls and got him to fires and scenes of crime so quickly and so often that the police must have had him on their list of suspects. And there was another colleague, John Salmon, the only Oxbridge import apart from myself, who had camouflaged his voice with layers of uniquely peculiar tones but still spoke riskily loudly in the way associated with toffs.

This played its part in an incident which clicked significantly with thoughts I was having at the time about the troubles encountered by black immigrants, who had so much to give to the north and were already refreshing its economy just as their Scottish or Jewish predecessors had done. John was working late not long after joining the paper when an elderly Bradfordian came into the newsroom and announced: 'I've brought the Nig Nog Notes.' John was already closely and beneficially involved in ethnic minority affairs in Manningham, but knew less about the music hall side of Bradford life: the Keith Waterhouse world of the Sunbeams, little children who would kill to get into the chorus of the Alhambra panto, the Churchill ladies luncheon clubs and of course the Nig Nogs. They were hugely popular children's clubs in the north, often particularly associated with cycling, but in general terms a non-uniform and less well-organised forerunner of the guides and scouts which required a lot of its little fans simply to tackle puzzles in a local newspaper column to try to win a badge. The name conjured up tribal images and an outdoor world of campfires and derring-do. When the *Northern Echo* in Darlington set up a Nig Nog Ring in 1929, 50,000 children joined within three months. Bradford's Nig Nogs were likewise invented by the *T&A* and although by 1975, the organisation was about to go the way of the Ovaltineys and Gypsy Romany's Chavvies of the Vardo, a few ancients such as John's late night note-deliverer clung on.

To John, however, nig nogs was more familiar as a nasty term of abuse, used on many of his neighbours in the streets of Bradford as part of the miserable vocabulary of prejudice. Whatever the supposed innocence of the club's origins, he would have suspected that an institutional racism underlay them, in the manner of the golliwog which still divides the country according to its context in childhood – jam jar label or playground sneer. There was a mismatch of minds, a row and both parties left feeling that the other was unpleasant and/ or stupid. This tallied with everything else I was seeing and reporting on – and, in a modest way, taking pains to avoid myself.

You can understand both points of view, but instead of condemning the mistakes of both the 'host' community and newcomers, let us celebrate instead the patience and goodwill that each has shown. John did marvellous work in the ethnically mixed area of Manningham and the Nig Nog man did the same with the city's young people. It is worth highlighting the virtues which have been common to both the settled community and the new settlers.

Like John, I lived in Manningham and enjoyed a year of particularly intense cosmopolitan life because the city council wanted to demolish my house and the other three terraces of fine Victorian buildings which stand round communal gardens off Lumb Lane and are called Southfield Square. The resulting campaign brought residents of 12 countries of origin together, with meetings in one of the two mosques, Sunni and Shia, which had been converted from two of the square's homes. Regardless of nationality, the resolution shown by everyone greatly struck me, even as I lost all chance of ever being slim again because of the number of compulsory teas laid on when I called to rally a neighbour or help with translating compulsory purchase warnings. But the three residents I most admired were two elderly women called Dorothea

Foster and Marjorie Townend, who were Bradford from birth and to the backbone. Miss Foster had worked at her namesake's mill, the famous John Fosters of Black Dyke in Queensbury, which won the national brass band competition so regularly that one of the frosted boardroom windows – frosted so that meetings could not be overlooked – was replaced with plain glass to display the virtually permanent trophy. Miss Townend had been at Brown Muff's, once Bradford's equivalent of Selfridges.

They had seen enormous changes in their surroundings, new neighbours speaking a different language, fewer old friends on their doorstep as 'white flight' took hold, and a sad decline in gardening in the centre of the square, something for which new arrivals from south Asia, working all hours, had neither the inclination nor the time. This especially irritated the third of my trio, a Ukrainian called Nancy Boychuck who was a living version of a matrioshka doll. She had lived in Southfield Square since the late 1940s and her garden was like something wonderful from a Russian fairy tale.

Nancy would berate her neighbours for their weed-infested plots, calling them 'naughty children' and threatening to have them 'sent to the Menster' which was her word for the huge West Riding psychiatric hospital at Menston, which has since been converted into housing for Leeds commuters. But she was not malicious and she gradually achieved results, although coriander and other herbs were usually her pupils' choice, rather than her own prolific flower borders and annually replanted prize dahlias. Like Miss Foster and Miss Townend, she was patient, looked to the long term and had faith that a varied community, for all the change and unfamiliarity involved, would add to Southfield Square's other virtues of being near shops and enclosing a green oasis within walking distance of town. We worked together, won our battle and the square is still there.

Taking Nancy's optimistic view deserves more credit than it sometimes gets, as do the very early efforts to welcome new communities, such as the Urdu articles which the *Telegraph & Argus* ran in the 1960s under an outstanding editor, Peter Harland, who went on to the *Sunday Times* as a lieutenant to another great journalist, Harold Evans, who made his name as editor of the *Northern Echo* in Darlington. It needs remembering that many of the people who found themselves with new and culturally completely different neighbours, were only in the first generation of enjoying a decent share of life's good things themselves. Few people are more tempted by prejudice than those who have recently escaped it. The progress of Jewish doctors in Leeds, for example, was hampered in the 1930s by suggestions that Irish families would not want them to treat their women. Judging by newspaper accounts, this was more rumour than demonstrable fact, but it was the sort of rumour which people were very ready to believe.

In spite of the progress made, patience on the part of immigrants sometimes seems required ad infinitum. Liverpool, for example, has an exceptionally long history of cosmopolitan communities because of its port, and they have often drawn admiring comment. As long ago as 1849, Herman Melville wrote in *Redburn: His First Voyage* about his experiences in the city a decade earlier: 'In Liverpool indeed the Negro steps with a prouder pace, and lifts his head like a man; for here, no such exaggerated feeling exists in respect of him, as in America.' Yet in an interview with Decca Aitkenhead in the *Guardian* in 2009, the actor Craig Charles recalled his teenage years in Liverpool, 130 years after Melville's time there, when he performed his poetry at the Everyman theatre:

'I was an angry young man, it was all poems about racism and the police and all that. I was writing poems about the riots, and it's funny how niggers don't show bruises, all this really hardcore stuff. It was about Liverpool at the time. Liverpool was a very racist place.'

I do not know any British Asian or Afro-Caribbean who has escaped some sort of racist treatment, and the hurt has been worse in many cases because it was so contrary to expectations. I remember being told by the Liberal peer Lord Navnit Dholakia, how his schoolbooks in India and Tanzania had led him to expect men to be wearing bowler hats when he arrived in the late 1950s to study at Brighton. He was genuinely surprised that they were not; and countless other immigrants' stories describe disillusion over more fundamental beliefs, especially discovering that the country which promoted itself as a mother and the home of fair play and democratic involvement was frequently none of these things. Lord Dholakia at least did better on the democratic involvement front. He went to try half a pint of beer at a Brighton pub (another essential of British behaviour according to his upbringing) and was approached by one

Muslim schoolboys in Dewsbury, 1989

of three students sitting at another table. They were Brighton Young Liberals, they told him, but they couldn't have a meeting without a quorum, which was four. Would he like to join them, and the party? He did both, which proved to be the first step to the Lords.

Dholakia's peerage has many parallels in the north, and that is a tribute to the persistence that its immigrants have shown, on top of the spirit of adventure and ambition – and sometimes desperation – common to all who leave their homeland for a new start. Another port, South Shields, is one of the most striking examples of this. During the late 1950s, when race riots became a familiar headline after a week of trouble in London at Notting Hill in August 1958, social commentators went to Shields to report on a place that had apparently found the answer. The *Shields Gazette* claimed that 'In no other part of the country has the problem been handled so well' and quoted local members of the Yemeni-origin community as saying: 'No colour bar here. Not even a colour problem here.'

Leeds' Caribbean Carnival, seen here in 1975, is only one year younger than Notting Hill's

My *Guardian* predecessor David Bean followed this up with a piece which concluded: 'Shields is a study in integration; a place where colour prejudice died years ago.' But both articles acknowledged that it had been a rocky road. The historian of the Yemeni community in Shields, Barry Carr, describes how racial conflict was so intense in 1919, at the end of the Merchant Navy manpower shortage which had led the government and shipowners to encourage Yemenis to come to Britain during the first world war, that the Durham Light Infantry had to intervene. A seamen's union official told Yemenis at the crew-hiring office on Mill Dam, a cobbled square by the Tyne: 'You black bastards, this ship is not for you,' and pitched battle ensued. There was a second one, again on the Mill Dam, 10 years later and in 1932, 38 Yemenis were marched between a double column of police to the railway station, to be deported as 'destitute aliens'. As late as 1950, a Pan-African Federation official said that Shields had 'a bad name all over the world among coloured people.'

And yet the communities did settle down. Councillors began to speak up for the Yemenis' virtues, one of them, a Conservative called Edmund Hill, helping a successful project to build a mosque with business advice. Victor Grunhut, a wealthy local solicitor who was himself an immigrant from Germany, gave both money and legal advice. There was a radical strain in Shields, not just from years of industrial struggle, but through comfortably-off locals such as Elinor Brent Dyer, whose hugely-popular *Chalet School* books were resolutely anti-Nazi and may have helped to link racist bullying on Tyneside with the horrors beginning to happen in Germany.

Barry Carr gives much of the credit, too, to the pragmatic, hard-working behaviour of the Yemenis, and this chimes with examples from immigrant communities all over the north. Thinking back to my own sense of excitement and enthusiasm as a young arrival in

Blending wool in Bradford for roof insulation

Bradford, it seems obvious and natural, and case after case in my work as a reporter has reinforced that view.

Errol James was an example, a young man who gave up his place at teacher training college in Jamaica to volunteer for the RAF during the second world war. After demob, he answered British government advertisements in Jamaican newspapers for factory work, to help the shattered economy's recovery, and thus came to Leeds. Out of uniform, which had largely protected him against racism, he encountered an ungrateful world of landladies' cards saying 'no coloureds' and all the small but grinding insults that are familiar to ethnic minorities. At his funeral in 1994 when he died at the age of 68, friends spoke of how this encouraged in him what they called a 'quiet rage' against such injustice. Mild by nature, he became relentless in working for change. He was a founder of the original Caribbean Cricket Club which used sport as a bridge to fair-minded locals. He encouraged the widest possible spectrum of colour and ethnicity in his colleagues on the Leeds branch of the International Council on Race Relations, forerunner of the succession of equality commissions later established by statute. With his wife Annese, and friends from his work as an engineering technician at Leeds University and his many interests outside, he worked for practical improvements, not gestures. After large-scale demonstrations against remaining colour-bar outposts, he would be found in quiet follow-up negotiations which brought such practices to an end.

Gertrude Paul was in the same mould, the first black headteacher in Leeds who also organised a Leeds University study of rehousing black people which was the standard text for over 20 years. She came to the city from St Kitts in 1956 in response to recruitment advertisements, after training in Antigua. She taught first in suburban schools but then as head of Elmhirst middle school in Chapeltown. Like Erroll, she was a founder and pillar of the United Caribbean Association and hostess to the Queen when UCA House was opened. She did Trojan work for the August Carnival which is only one year younger than Notting Hill's and involves the same spectacular festival of sequins, food and sound. She helped calm young people during periods of trouble – another of Erroll's quiet specialities – and she did not forget her roots. She paid a memorable visit back to her home village of Parson's Ground with new hospital equipment, bought through fund-raising by the St Kitts community in Leeds.

The Irish who were forced to hide in the dark behind curtains after Lord Mountbatten's death, showed the same practical attitude. They met and decided: we need to involve ourselves with the community. No one's going to abuse our kids, so let's join the carnival with a float. They did, that year, and won a prize.

And then there was Mohammed Ajeeb, whom I first met during the battle for Southfield Square, when he was working for a Bradford offshoot of the housing charity Shelter and clearly not enjoying the north's winter weather. Most of our tactical planning took place in his small office warmed to furnace levels by sitting as close as we could to a three-bar electric fire. Ajeeb was the third child of a village carpenter in Mirpur. He left at 16 for Karachi, working on building sites to pay for a BA course locally, before coming to Britain in 1957 with a fiver and the address of some student friends in Nottingham. He finished up as lord mayor of Bradford in 1989, the first British Asian to hold the position, but he needed plenty of perseverance. For 10 years after he joined the Labour party in 1968, he kept missing out on the chance to fight a council seat because ward committees saw Asians as vote-losers. 'At least one side of the Rushdie affair was that it really involved the community in politics,' he told me, when I met him and his wife Arshad to congratulate them on their daughter Rizwana embarking on a law and sociology degree. It was a welcome transfer of energies which had previously focused more on politics in Pakistan. In the year of the book burning, I went to talk to activists at the Pakistan People's Party office in Bradford, squashed between an old mill wall and the derelict Britannia social club. Ayoub Mirza, one of the main men, prodded me in in the stomach repeatedly, saying: 'You are happy Benazir win? You be happy!' But he was also ready to lecture me knowledgeably on doorstep, Bradford matters.

Getting stuck in like that was also the whole point for Abdul Shaif, who at 28 was secretary of the Yemeni community association in Sheffield and introduced me to members of the Yemeni Stars XI football team at the end of the 1980s. He talked about the way that sheer hard work had discouraged his father's generation from similar ways of getting to know Sheffielders beyond their own community. Shaif senior came to the north in 1959, in response to recruiting advertisements in Aden. 'Their work was the hardest,' said Abdul.

Hadrian's garrison included African and Syrian troops

'Sixty hours a week was ordinary, 90 or more quite common. They shared rooms, all worked in steel, had no time for language lessons after work and hadn't been to school under British colonial rule. No wonder the community kept to itself for years, invisible really to the rest of the city.' For some of his father's generation, steelmaking terms such as slinger, sweepings or ingot were still their only non-Arabic words, after so many years. Abdul and his friends were different, indeed their integration had been canny. They were strong supporters of the miners' strike, although the biggest portrait on the community centre wall was not of Arthur Scargill but of Abdul Fattah Ismail, who led the rebellion against British colonial rule in south Yemen.

These were work contacts. At home, we have got to know Lashman Singh, who runs a chimney-sweeping service but also organises a meals-for-the-elderly charity called the Curry Project in his spare time. He talks fascinatingly about both as his automatic sweeping system hums away under a ghostly covering of sheets. He started his

Working on sustainable allotments in Chorlton, Manchester

working life as a building mason but found that he was forever unblocking old flues, as people reverted to open fires. Chimney enthusiasm took hold of him. He took City and Guilds courses and won a set of national vocational training qualifications. In no time, he was an executive member of the National Association of Chimney Sweeps. I went up on a vast mansion's roof with him to do a piece about his school for sweeps, which used three fake chimneys with a bewildering range of flues to teach the trade.

Up the road, there's Gurnham Singh Chana, who sells the cheapest quality plants in Leeds from racks which fill the pavement outside his corner shop in Nether Yeadon. Custom has been so intense – and appreciated – that Leeds highways people have altered the roadside kerb to allow more parking. Chana, his wife Narinda Khaur and their 24-year-old son Sunny wheel more than 60 trolleys outside every day, an enterprise which has grown from a modest request by a neighbour, when the corner shop was just a conventional place

A human moment at the battle of Orgreave in 1984, as picket George Brealey and PC Paul Castle catch one another's eye DON MCPHEE

John Dalton forever collecting marsh gas in Manchester town hall
FORD MADOX BROWN / BRIDGEMAN

Sheep run through the famous landscape of Wensleydale at Mile House farm near Hawes, 2008 CHRISTOPHER THOMOND

The Royal Liverpool Philharmonic orchestra plays Liverpool – the Musical in the new Echo Arena at the opening of the city's year as European Capital of Culture 2008
CHRISTOPHER THOMOND

Burnsall near Bolton Abbey in Wharfedale. Even in winter, a green and lovely spot
DON MCPHEE

Dr Johnson, William Wordsworth and Thomas Carlyle are among 60 worthies honoured in John Rylands Library, Manchester, funded by the cotton magnate's Anglo-Cuban widow, Enriqueta DON MCPHEE

Cricket in the evening by Lister's Mill, Bradford, whose silk-weaving sheds are being converted into flats and urban lofts CHRISTOPHER THOMOND

Tyneside transformed by the Sage and Millennium 'winking' bridge DON MCPHEE

A riot of marble in Leeds' Victoria Quarter where Harvey Nichols' store has taken more pro rata than its counterpart in Knightsbridge, London DON MCPHEE

Diners walk up Skiddaw, England's fourth highest mountain, for a three course meal in a temporary restaurant at Keswick's 2008 Mountain Festival
CHRISTOPHER THOMOND

selling groceries, to see if the family could shift three trays of home-grown primroses. Every plant was sold by 10am that day, and Chana recognised a business opportunity which has since prospered further with Sunny opening a second outlet in Saltaire, five miles away. There had been no resentment when the family took over the long-established old shop, either, of the sort that smeared Jews in Leeds in 1930 with allegations that they were converting their homes into secret businesses. No one else was willing to risk a business so close to Yeadon Morrisons, half-a-mile up Henshaw Lane. If it hadn't been for the Chanas, the shop would have closed after 137 years' trade.

We all benefit. And a welcome to immigrants pays long-term dividends, beyond the prosperity and jobs which their enterprise creates, in the affection which so many have given back to the north when they have made good. The Burtons from Lithuania, the Alliances from Iran – and one of my own favourites, the Nobel Laureate from Nigeria, Wole Soyinka. He studied English in Leeds from 1954-7 and stayed on in the city for two years, writing his first important plays there, *The Swamp Dwellers* and *The Lion and the Jewel*. Since then, he has returned repeatedly to give readings, encourage young playwrights and premier work at the West Yorkshire Playhouse, rather than London or New York in the manner of Sir Alan Ayckbourn, based in Scarborough. There is a modest investment which has brought rich returns, and that's the sort of deal northerners like.

7

The Cultural Hold of Gloom

'The heart of the north is dead, and its fingers
are corpse fingers.'
DH Lawrence, 'Letter to JM Murray' 1924

I f you are wondering what sort of sexual misery inspired DH Lawrence to write the above, I can put you right immediately. He was writing about the weather. He needed to go south for warmth, he added in the letter, and of course he did, not merely to the south of England but to Sicily and eventually New Mexico.

Lawrence's eminence might be enough to make me throw in the towel when it comes to challenging the centuries of cultural prejudice about the north, except though his home territory of Nottinghamshire scarred him for life, he gave us plenty of balancing descriptions about his despoiled but still beautiful part of Nottinghamshire. Mellors and Lady Chatterley found some exquisite sylvan nooks to canoodle in, and their real-life successors are vigorously defending them against open-cast mining as this book goes to print. Anyway, was he wrong about our weather?

I would not go so far as the Book of Job, which tells us that 'Fair weather cometh out of the north', but the real divide between warmth and chill in England is between west and east. Our island is much too small and temperate to have serious climatic differences of any sort, but I would rather spend a November or February afternoon on the sheltered streets of Lytham St Annes, or pottering round Arnside, than in the knife-edge winds of Cambridge or Southend-on-Sea.

Like most things in Britain, the weather pattern is complicated and differences depend on very local circumstances. In the admittedly likely event of your getting caught by rain in the Lake District, the best option if practicable is to head for another valley. I have walked in sunshine all day round Ullswater while friends were getting drenched in Little Langdale. The fall in temperature as you travel England's small contribution of miles towards the North Pole is very gradual and there are lots of anomalies such as the fact that Newcastle upon Tyne in January is on average warmer than the Thames valley. Leeds is drier than Barcelona.

I call those 'anomalies', but to do so is to slip into DH Lawrence's cast of mind. During the snows of February 2009, my wife and I drove back from London to Leeds on a Sunday evening and before Luton we already had plump snowflakes whirling into the windscreen in what appeared to be solid lines. Two hundred miles of this would have been wearing and possibly foolish, even though we had our rugs and Thermos plus a shovel in the boot. But then we looked at one another and said simultaneously: 'But it isn't going to get worse. It's going to get better.' This wasn't optimistic northern loyalty but the reassurance of checking out the forecast online before we set off. Even so, we had almost slipped into the conventional assumption that the weather will always be worse up north. And this was in spite of the fact that I had spent the weekend mocking an email from the *Guardian* to all staff on the Friday appealing for early copy because

Is it always winter (and raining) in the north?

'our friends in the north [groan] have snow.' We hadn't, didn't and weren't expecting to. The sun was shining out of a cloudless blue sky as I read the message and it had been all day.

I have a sturdy ally. Within months of returning to the north in 1987 to write about Yorkshire and the north-east for the *Guardian*, I started receiving postcards of northern beauty spots or celebrated northerners, gently correcting my mistakes in looping black biro which looked as though it was always about to run out of ink. The writer had none of the righteous tone which often accompanies readers' complaints, a tone which is understandable given our error-ridden profession. Far from getting at me, my critic was gentle and instructive, clearly wanting to help me avoid pitfalls in the future and to add to my stock of northern knowledge.

But two things about the cards were intriguing and slightly annoying. They were always anonymous, which reduces credibility, and they came from Welwyn Garden City, which I do not regard as being in the north. I have already made clear my hesitations about northern exiles who write about the region as though time stopped on the day they departed. Mystery Person was not out of date like that, far from it: although he lived in distant Hertfordshire he was so confoundedly knowledgeable and right. I discovered the answer when, by chance, I noticed a letter about the north one day in the *Guardian's* correspondence column. It was short and good natured, came from Welwyn and the name on it was Alan Myers. The rest was easy. Myers is an exile but one well-known in the north and the north-east particularly, especially in cultural circles which he explores with erudition and wit. His essays such as the nicely-entitled 'Priestley being Beastly', in the short-lived intellectual quarterly *Northern Review*, show a thorough knowledge of the way writers have treated the north, especially the north-east. He squirrels out the obscurest examples of visiting commentators getting everything hopelessly wrong, as well as a rather smaller number of heroes who get them right.

Myers has a particular passion about the distortion of northern weather, on which he is a one-man version of the Meteorological Office. If I ever mention in an article that drizzle surrounded Haworth or that Nissan workers gathered in Sunderland on a dour day, a postcard of somewhere northern in midsummer arrives, accompanied by devastating statistics. I got the Thames valley one from him. Ditto the fact that Oxford and Cambridge have longer periods when the temperature falls below freezing than Manchester.

Myers uses this data in *north & SOUTH*, a satirical manual of correct behaviour for metropolitan or southern journalists when describing conditions in the north. Based on years of recording actual usage, his instructions range from the obvious – always highlighting bad weather – to the more subtle ways in which pleasant conditions are presented as surprising. As he puts it: 'If the sun is actually shining when you visit, use a formula such as 'Mercifully the rain has held off'. He is right to claim that gardening discussions from the north often do mention the wind, cold or wet three times in the first 10 minutes. And there are plenty of examples of metropolitan media expeditions to beautiful places being gleefully timed for when they are at their rare worst. As Beryl Bainbridge says concisely during a film-making project, in one of Myers' examples: 'Who but a TV crew would go to Tynemouth beach in October?'

Perpetual drizzle in our 24-hour media naturally influences attitudes, but southern weatherism goes back a long way. Coketown in Dickens's *Hard Times* is denied its fair share of the sun that shines on its real-life model, Preston. Dotheboys Hall in *Nicholas Nickleby*, which Dickens placed at Greta Bridge in the gentle countryside of

Bleakness in Batley, 1973

Teesdale, is perpetually as bleak and chilling as its name. Myers' microscope detects the tendency everywhere. The Australian novelist Christina Stead produced a classically bleak portrait of Tyneside in a novel called *Cotter's England*, where the usual malign descriptions of filthy industry and stunted lives are compounded by the story being set in a dismally cold and wet February. And yet she went to Newcastle upon Tyne to do her research in the summer of 1949, which the diligent Myers has established was notably warm. What a shame that she didn't follow the cheery approach of another writer, Baron Avro Manhattan, who liked South Shields and the walk to its pier so much, that he and his wife bought their third home there after visiting several times. The others were in Kensington and Spain.

I have called the rain-soaked approach southern weatherism, but it is also the work of a northern fifth column which includes names as distinguished as that of Lawrence. Most notably, does the sun ever shine or the wind stop howling round Wuthering Heights? Is Mrs

Gaskell's Manchester often bathed in light and warmth (as opposed to Cranford, which has a much better micro-climate, although not far down the A34 in Cheshire)? There isn't too much sunlight either in the northern stages of JB Priestley's *English Journey* although he has the decency to explain to his readers why some places get it in the neck. When he slags Newcastle off in a way he would never do to his native Bradford, he admits that he arrived in the city feeling lousy on a November day when rain and wind, as well as fog, had drifted up the Tyne.

There is something deeply rooted in this psychology; the voluntary promotion by northerners of damaging images which are nonetheless 'gritty' or 'tough' and so chime with the Hovis advert feeling – pride in overcoming origins as bleak as the hearts that beat in those who overcame them were warm. It is no surprise that the filming of those masterpieces of the cobbles and brass band genre were the work of a young South Shields graduate of Hartlepool school of art, Ridley Scott, who went on to the Royal College of Art, where one day he borrowed a Bolex 16mm camera, and made a short film that set him back £65 but set him on the path to fame as a Hollywood director of movies including *Blade Runner*, *Gladiator*, and *Black Hawk Down*. But they cried out for the almost equally famous take on them in the *Monty Python* sketch The Three Yorkshiremen, whose characters vie to outdo one another in tales of an upbringing where all manner of things could be bought for a farthing ('And you still got change') even if you did live in a cardboard box.

One of the northern bibles of this school is a book which greatly distresses me, although it has fine photographs and stimulating text. It is called *The Essential West Riding* by Herbert Whone, who was once a guide at Fountains Abbey, one of the most beautiful places in the world, and is therefore all the more culpable for his relentless

Hovisry. Priestley wrote the foreword for the original 1974 book, but my 1987 edition is introduced by the former prime minister, Harold Wilson, who used another of the north's loveliest places, Rievaulx in North Yorkshire, when he came to choose a title in the House of Lords. In his introduction for Mr Whone he writes lyrically and accurately of his boyhood scout camps 'away from the smoke' up the Holme valley between Meltham and Honley, and later in Rievaulx itself, the mellow stones of the ancient abbey and the gentle landscape of North Yorkshire.

Is there any of this in *The Essential West Riding* itself? None. Rievaulx is disqualified by the ridings' boundaries, but there ought to be space for Merrydale – a name which speaks for itself – and the other pretty Pennine spots where child Harold scouted. They and their equivalents in places such as the Midgehole valley where Halifax boy scouts spent – and still spend – idyllic summer days, are every bit as essential to my county as mill chimneys. And even the latter can and should be shown in their frequently beautiful context. If I want to have my breath taken away, I drive to my sister's house in Shipley over the shoulder of 600ft Carr Hill in Wrose, where the road swoops down above the confluence of the Aire valley and Bradford beck in a zigzag with huge, uninterrupted views.

First you take in the wooded hillside of Manningham and Heaton, dotted with Victorian spires and towers and crowned by Lister's former velvet mill, whose chimney was so large that the board of directors planked over the shaft and had a banquet at the topping-out. Small wonder the place is being converted into posh flats by the Manchester developers, Urban Splash. Then the road snakes 90 degrees and the whole panorama of the Aire valley opens out below, plenty more chimneys and another Titanic mill, where Sir Titus Salt made the world's finest mohair, again surrounded by greenery and indeed picturesque crags below a school which is aptly called Ladderbanks. Much of this vista is a world heritage site like Fountains Abbey. Look in vain for such impressions in Whone.

Instead, text and especially photos portray a black-and-white world which seems for the most part plunged in perpetual winter like the white witch's Narnia or the realm of the Snow Queen, only darker. Broken mill windows are reflected in puddles between setts or cobbles, preferably with litter nearby. Scarcely a tree is in leaf. When I came to a poem called 'Ode to Summer' and muttered 'Glory be!' out loud, I found it referred to thunder and lightning, matched its sunshine with showers and even contained the lines:

'As from the noisy tadpole
We hear the crackin' din.'

Part of me wondered what William Wright was on in 1876, when

Fountains Abbey, where Herbert Whone was a guide

Brontëland. Hard to let cheerfulness in

he published this in a collection called *Random Rhymes and Rambles*. But I am also convinced that he did not want any suggestion that a northern summer was a pansy affair like a southern one. He reinforces my suspicions by his pen-name which exactly meets southerners' requirements of such a bard: Bill o' th' Hoylus End.

There is even a photograph of Knaresborough which manages to make that lovely place look dour, partly by giving too much prominence to the massive old viaduct imposed on the place in 1848 by the West Yorkshire Junction Railway, whose directors must have had the same frame of mind as Bill o' th' Hoylus End. I am especially sad about this, as Knaresborough is one of the key destinations on my the-north-is-not-what-you-thought tour for visitors from elsewhere. The town is like an Italian coastal village in the Cinque Terra, brightly coloured houses tumbling down mellow cliffs amid luxuriant foliage. At the bottom is the Nidd not the Med, but the effect is the same; people dipping their toes in the water, splashing around in rowing boats (so many that you sometimes can hardly see the surface of the river) and eating ice-creams in the hot sun. If you think I am exaggerating, note that the unimpeachable Sir Simon Jenkins recently compared Knaresbrough to French towns high above the Dordogne.

To be fair to the wider school of northern writers, it is not always the case that they exclude such idyllic scenes from their work. It is more that the reader does not notice them because the wilder and darker passages are so much more characterful and different. I referred to Brontë descriptions of warmth and light in Chapter 5, and here is another: Jane Eyre coming to Thornfield on a far from wuthering day when Rochester's estate is enjoying a roasting summer. The roads have lost their mud and turned white and baked, the meadows have dried out and become parched like those in Tuscany or the Romagna. Charlotte Brontë writes: 'A splendid midsummer shone over England; skies so pure, suns so radiant as were then seldom seen in long succession, seldom favour even singly our wave-girt land. It was as if a band of Italian days had come from the south like a flock of glorious passenger birds...' She is not to be dissuaded from the view that such weather is rare in England as a whole, but at least she allows the northern fastnesses of her novel to share in it.

Some years ago, I was talking about this to the writer Dr Juliet Barker, who had just been appointed as curator of the Brontë Parsonage museum. She had announced her pleasure in getting the Brontë Society to agree to a thorough spring clean, and I wanted to write about this as it accorded with my own way of thinking. 'People are so keen for the Brontë world to be dark,' she said, as we tut-tutted together in the famous old vicarage's light rooms with their lovely views. Much respected as a Brontë scholar, with books as big as doorstops to prove it, she gave me the chapter and verse to support my instincts about sisters whose imaginations were so lively and whose childhood books about the fictional country of Angria so full of zest. Some of her startlingly modern-looking redecoration included wallpaper which might have been designed by Laura Ashley but was actually copied from a scrap of the original found in Charlotte's desk. 'A lot of visitors seem to want gloom at the Parsonage,' said Barker, 'but for almost 30 years this was a happy family home.'

That didn't convince a lot of her customers. Staff at the Parsonage had to pacify tourists who wanted to know what had happened to the 'nice dark paint and wallpaper' and my report triggered demands to 'bring back the gloom.' One letter-writer suggested that the wallpaper fragment might have been smuggled into Charlotte's desk by a more recent visitor. I must admit that I had a sneaking sympathy with him, because his first visit to Haworth had been an authentically wuthering experience. It coincided with a thunderstorm which drove him to shelter in the Parsonage as the trees in the graveyard rocked, sending rooks spiralling up into the bucketing rain. Only the Laura Ashley effect let him down.

The treatment of light is another aspect of the tendency to treat the north as so often essentially dark. Even supporters of the region use Alfred, Lord Tennyson's lines from *The Princess*,

> '... bright ... is the south,
> And dark and true and tender is the north.'

although this is addressed to a swallow, and its north is the whole of northern Europe, compared to a south consisting of the bird's African wintering grounds. Mundanely, the only justification for the darkists is northern geology rather than psyche. We suffer from the curse of sandstone in the region's busiest areas which attract the attention of writers because of the greater possibilities for human drama. It is an unlucky coincidence that the dominant building material, millstone grit, darkens with age exacerbated by soot. If only more masterpieces of literature had been set in the Eden valley of Cumbria, where the stone is a warm, pinkish red. Or on the magnesian limestone which runs from east of Sheffield to north of York. I have already highlighted Sir Walter Scott's paean to the latter landscape in *Ivanhoe* but it is a lonely example. Another famous book almost gave it a hand, *The Water Babies*, in which Charles Kingsley shows admirable fair play between the ordeal of the little hero's working life and the beautiful countryside to which he escapes. Both settings are northern, the second based on Malham and the mysterious source of the river Aire which remains wonderful today, a combination of prettiness and the grandeur of the Cove and Gordale Scar. But unfortunately, *The Water Babies'* wholesome influence is limited because the action soon moves underwater and stays there.

A more balanced portfolio of geological settings would mitigate the great soot problem described in Chapter 1. There was no doubting this, and since writing that section, I have been rereading Corinne Silva's history of the Irish diaspora in Leeds, which has plenty to add. The memories from the 1950s of Mary from County Mayo, for example, are headlined 'The blackest place', drawn from her first shocked impression: 'I remember thinking "My God, this is the blackest place. The buildings were very black and the trams were trundling."' It's true; I remember that as well, but it isn't the case any more. For today's visitors, the glass towers of Manchester, Leeds and Liverpool make that clear straight away. Whatever their merits or otherwise as architecture, they are light.

That is a change, but not as fundamental a one as we may think.

The Brontës' view from Haworth parsonage

'Northern lights' have a much longer pedigree than the architecture of the last 30 years. They long pre-date initiatives such as Operation Eyesore which scrubbed the whole of Windhill in Shipley clean in 1972, turning the place honey-coloured within the space of a couple of months, from its previous black. I am probably biased, because my great-great-grandfather was nicknamed Leeds' 'smoke king' by the *Yorkshire Evening News* because of a patent which he designed and installed in Victorian factory chimneys. But as soon as I returned in 1988, I started discovering examples of buildings by the fresh air and light school of early 20th-century architecture which did much pioneering in the north.

A large and obvious example is Port Sunlight at the tip of the Wirral, the determinedly open, airy and healthy housing commissioned by Lord Leverhulme who wanted his workers' village to be as clean and bright as the soap after which it was named. Less obvious are the interiors of the metaphorically 'dark' mills, both cotton and woollen. Light floods into them from windows whose size was a sensational advance in 19th-century architecture, or from toplights which include, at Marshall's former flax mill in Leeds, elegant domes surrounded by one of the country's first turf roofs. The grass was cropped by half-a-dozen sheep until one of them fell through a dome.

My favourite is much more modest. As you enter Castleford from Featherstone, you pass an exquisite building which I toured some years ago in the course of writing a piece about fresh air schools. Formerly Whitwood Mere primary, since converted to be an outstation of York University, it forms a beautiful curve designed to face the sun. Each of the classrooms in the crescent has wall-to-floor windows which were removed entirely on warm days. They led on to gardens which the children tended. Each internal door has two porthole windows, one at teacher- and one at child-height and the architect Oliver Hill, who built the school in 1939-40, incorporated an equally light-hearted, incised faience frieze of animals by John Skeaping, Barbara Hepworth's first husband. This was a West Riding school, as was my own sons' comprehensive, Benton Park in Rawdon, which actually suffered from too much light. Our parent teacher association had to raise funds to pay for a special shading film to cover the many floor-to-ceiling windows, because the glare of summer sunshine made classrooms uncomfortably hot. We had to darken that little bit of the north.

Such pioneering buildings were the work of architects from all over the country but their raison d'être was significantly developed in the north, at classes conducted by the stylish head of the school of architecture at Liverpool University, Sir Charles Reilly. A man with matinée-idol looks, a black felt hat and more often than not a cane, he had a habit of collaring students arriving for interviews with other departments and persuading them that architecture was their real aim in life. One such was an 18-year-old called Stirrat Johnson-Marshall who was ambushed in a train to Manchester, where he hoped to study civil engineering, by what he described as 'a plump gentleman wearing a black coat and broad-brimmed hat.' It was Reilly, who gave his usual pitch so eloquently that Johnson-Marshall changed his mind and applied to Liverpool. His interviewer was the same plump gentleman, and he was accepted.

Reilly's many works included cottages in Port Sunlight and Johnson-Marshall took the gospel on to many other local authorities, including the London County Council. The West Riding's education officer Sir Alec Clegg also seized the reins and commissioned expensive architects to get the best work. Sir Basil Spence of Coventry Cathedral designed comprehensives in Sheffield and my sons' over-light school was the work of Sir John Burnet, Tait and Partners, whose British

Museum court flanking the reading room has just been gently shaded with great panache by Norman Foster.

Spence was back in the north again for Sunderland city council when they decided to build a civic centre in 1970. Widely considered to be the best of the 20th century's collection of these 'town halls for the future,' it is an almost Babylonian complex of gentle terraces, indoor galleries and tumbling plants, all flooded with light. Spence created a pattern of hexagons which he described as 'informal and allowing free pedestrian movement to all parts.' The centre looks open, transparent and democratic, all qualities associated with light, and Sunderland has now followed it up with a dazzling Winter Gardens by Napper Architects. Sheffield has done the same, Pringle Richards Sharratt roofing part of the centre with great arches of laminated wood, supporting glass panes above palm trees on the scale of Kew Gardens' temperate and tropical houses. Hull has an extraordinary,

Sunshine and warmth at Port Sunlight

mega-aquarium by Sir Terry Farrell shaped like a shark with its eye a glazed restaurant overlooking the Humber (which like my sons' school, has the one flaw of sometimes becoming unbearably hot). David Chipperfield's Hepworth gallery opens in Wakefield in 2011, with more great windows opening on to one of the landscapes which inspired Dame Barbara's work. Leeds has added to its Victorian arcades by roofing streets in two separate areas, one of them actually rebranded as The Light.

By day, this is like another vast greenhouse but it is light at night too, with a series of colours which change in a sequence. The same applies to Wilkinson Eyre's graceful Winking Bridge across the Tyne between Newcastle and its twin city, Gateshead, which is also the home of Lord Foster's curving, glass-panelled Sage concert hall which glows in the dark. My wife Penny tells me that the glass floor-to-ceiling wall of the ladies at the neighbouring Baltic Arts Centre is a wonder of the world, although I cannot vouch for that in person. All these cities run lighting award competitions and the countryside puts on its own spectacular too. We have night-time, just as they do in the south, but it comes spangled with the gold and silver of house and street lights which is exceptionally visible, and beautiful, in the hilly areas which form so much of the north. My brother-in-law, a contented transplant from London, describes the experience of driving at night above the Pennine towns as like flying at night, and so it is. The writer Phyllis Bentley was struck in a similar, memorable way by seeing the trams pioneering up the hillsides at night, and comparing them to jewelled beetles.

Pleasant weather, bright light – and something else is missing from the broken mirror of the north too often held up to the world. You remember how when Alan Myers drew up his rules in *north & SOUTH*, he instructed metropolitan journalists never to describe middle class northerners enjoying the sort of comfort or culture taken for granted by their counterparts in London? Like all his suggestions, this is a major exaggeration, but you do not need to spend much time in the company of impresarios such as Ian Brown of the West Yorkshire Playhouse, or his predecessor Jude Kelly, or Dame Fanny Waterman of the Leeds International Piano Competition, to sense the frustration and stress involved in trying to catch national attention.

It is not an unwillingness or the prejudice imagined by Myers which is usually responsible for this, but the lack of staff, of resources to station enough regular national reviewers in the region (and all other regions, apart from Greater London). And here you may sympathise with London editors and their finite budgets, because of the sheer scale of the cultural offering in the north. Huddersfield stages the country's best contemporary music festival; York and Beverley have excellent early music ones. Sir Mark Elder maintains the Hallé Orchestra at the breathtaking standard it has enjoyed for most of its 151 years. Liverpool has the Phil, Newcastle the Northern Sinfonia, Sheffield the string tradition exemplified for 40 years until their retirement in 2005 by the Lindsay Quartet. Opera North repeatedly wins plaudits for the daring of its productions as well as their quality, to the extent that a suggestion in the spring of 2009 that a northern arm of the Royal Opera House should be created in Manchester met a lukewarm response. The fear was that it might damage the already successful home team and rob the equally successful Lowry Centre in Salford of audience. In theatre, the two most frequently-performed playwrights after Shakespeare, Sir Alan Ayckbourn and John Godber, are based respectively at Scarborough and Hull. Manchester has the Royal Exchange theatre, Liverpool the Everyman and even little Keswick the Theatre by the Lake, successfully developed from the Century Theatre's old Blue Box, a collection of lorries which deployed like a wagon train in the 1950s to take theatre all over the country. They came to rest in Keswick in 1976 but moved to Snibston in Leicestershire when the Theatre by the Lake was built in 1996. Art galleries abound, not only the excellent municipal collections in galleries such as the Laing in Newcastle or the Walker in Liverpool. You will also find the biggest collection of David Hockney's work in the world at Saltaire, close to his native Bradford. And the Woodhorn Museum on a former colliery site in Northumberland has a similar world's-biggest devoted to the Ashington Group of painters. They were off-duty miners who organised an adult education group in 1934 and chose art appreciation as a subject because it 'sounded interesting'. After a lecture on Michelangelo stimulated little interest, their tutor Robert Lyon from Durham University, suggested that they have a go themselves at painting. The results led to high praise from national critics. There is also a rich collection of national museums in the north: railways at York, media in Bradford, the Tate in Liverpool, the Imperial War Museum North in Salford and the *de facto* national medical museum at the Thackray in Leeds.

Yet there are grounds for concern well illustrated by the work of the French photographer Marc Riboud. In 1954 Riboud was sent on assignment to the north of England after an instructive discussion in the office of Len Spooner, picture editor of the celebrated magazine *Picture Post*. Riboud was a novice but one with a powerful patron in Robert Capa, the great war photographer and a much-valued contributor to *Picture Post*, who was also at the meeting. Riboud was aiming high in hoping to get an assignment with the magazine, but *Picture Post* was running a series of photographic essays on Britain's cities and Spooner couldn't find anyone who wanted to do the one he had scheduled for Leeds. 'Marc is the very man for you,' Capa told him, seizing the unexpected chance for his inexperienced friend. 'He himself comes from Lyons, the dreariest city in France.'

It was a back-handed compliment but it got Riboud the job, and the results were anything but boring. The pictures showed a grimy but lively community, swarming with grubby but well-fed, welfare state kids, and the accompanying text was unusually even-handed. It did full justice to the omnipresence of soot but also acknowledged the beauty of the nearby countryside and the exceptional number of well-tended parks. What was missing then? Well, us. My four-year-old self, my family and the tens of thousands like us who lived in the middling part of the city. But in the spring of 2009 an exhibition was held at the new Leeds City Museum of Riboud's 1954 pictures, side-by-side with a second set taken by the now very famous Magnum photographer in 2005, commissioned by the *Guardian*. The co-curator Janet Douglas of Leeds Metropolitan University gave a lively lecture on the subject, and she couldn't have been clearer. 'The middle class suburbs did not interest him,' she told a meeting of the overwhelmingly middle class Leeds Philosophical & Literary Society, whose members all nodded with middle class understanding. 'To him they were boring, the same as in so many other cities.'

This was borne out by the 2005 images, few of which had anything like the power of those taken in 1954. Riboud was much older, but the difference was in the subject, not the technique. The modern photographs were in colour, but their relative failure to excite was not because they lacked the stark contrasts of 1954's black and white. They were mostly taken in the city centre and they showed it as it is – lively, colourful, busy, modern. And therefore very much like city centres all over the world. Even on the way out of the exhibition, where I hadn't bothered to search for my youthful self because I knew that I wouldn't be there, I found myself struggling to recall what the 2005 portfolio had shown.

Quarrying stone for London's Regent Street near Huddersfield

But it was closer to the whole truth than his earlier expedition. When he visited in 1954, Janet told us, Riboud presented himself as a documentary photographer, but his documents had left those middle class pages almost blank. The grimy street urchins and the washing slung across the back-to-back terraces were so much more compelling and, to be fair, so much more distinctive, than suburbia. But the wider context was absent. It is very hard to get this balance right and still be interesting and creative, but there is one magnificent success in the world of art which I use to illustrate talks on journalism. Because there, too, we face great difficulty in placing the unusual – and therefore newsworthy – event in the larger but generally more boring sum of things.

The exception is Pieter Bruegel the Elder's painting in the Musée des Beaux Arts in Brussels, *Landscape with the Fall of Icarus* – and the words 'landscape with' are crucial. More than 99 per cent of the painting shows a farmer ploughing, a shepherd leaning on his stick, the sunshine catching a distant city and a merchant ship ploughing out to sea. So where is the boy with the melted wings? Look at the ship's wake, and there is the lower part of one slender leg sticking out of the sea and a few sorry feathers floating nearby. That is the drama, everything else is the context, and Bruegel is one of the very few people to achieve a masterpiece with these two components in the right proportion. The point is well reinforced in WH Auden's poem on the painting, 'Musée des Beaux Arts':

> 'About suffering they were never wrong,
> The Old Masters; how well, they understood
> Its human position; how it takes place
> While someone else is eating or opening a window or
>   just walking dully along.'

Without the context, endless subtleties are lost. A modern traveller may glance, for instance, at a meadow near Berwick on Tweed and find it southern in its gentle Englishness. But a quadrat will reveal the absence of species you would find in Sussex and their replacement by different ones, native to Northumberland. This is not exclusive to perceptions of the north, except perhaps for the way they have lasted so long, and show such stubbornness in persisting. False impressions have been given of other parts of the country, but they have either been changed by time, or the area itself has changed to make them justifiable. Consider Dorset, the county of Thomas Hardy, whose lyrical writing made common cause with the landscape to create an Eden; one where bad things happened, but on nothing like the scale that he knew to be real: iron oppression by church and squire, labourers turning to unions and strikes, and emigration as the only alternative to starving, which saw Hardy's own cousins sail reluctantly to the United States. I turned on the TV in the spring of 2009 to see Jeremy Paxman making this very point about the olde English countryside as a whole. 'Five million people emigrated in the second half of the 19th century,' he told us, and he has reason to feel the argument personally. When his roots were examined in another TV programme, *Who Do You Think You Are?*, he discovered how his own family left the jobless farming world of East Anglia for the mills of Lancashire during the Industrial Revolution. They travelled more like goods than people, men, women and children, each with a number, on canal boats which delivered them to the factories' wharves. From gentle south to tough north, perhaps. But also from destitution to a living.

If Hardy's lasting images draw us to Dorset today, we discover them to have become generally true. The old hovels are desirable rural homes, Dorchester is spick and span and Prince Charles has chosen the county for his miniature Utopia at Poundbury near Dorchester. But if we look diligently, we can also find modern versions of the misery of Hardy's time, in off-season lodging houses round Bournemouth and Weymouth, or among the 11,891 young people (in 2008 and likely to be more now) in households classified as below the poverty line. The county council helpfully publishes maps in varying shades of green which show speckles of viridian – the worst level – against softer colours which chart the comfortably or well-off. Perhaps their staff should have a go at writing novels that tell the full story.

At one time, this seemed to be the answer for the north. The northern battalion of the 1950s' new wave fiction was a crack force – John Braine, Stan Barstow, David Sillitoe, Keith Waterhouse, Willis Hall. They had the old northern backdrop all right; Penguin Books reassured prospective readers of *Room at the Top* that its hero Joe Lampton had been properly 'raised in poverty and squalor in an ugly north country town.' But their most effective characters such as Lampton and Waterhouse's Billy Fisher (aka Liar) were characteristic of the revivified new north in their energy and belief that the good things of life were available locally and therefore within their reach. After succeeding and moving to London, Waterhouse in particular made a refreshing decision. He was tired of being typecast by the London literary world as a northern writer and turned consciously against the restrictive niche after an evening at JB Priestley's flat in the early 1960s. The Old Grumbler, as Waterhouse nicknames him, had assembled a collection of authors who had been described to him as the northern wing of John Osborne's band of 'angry young men.'

'Angry are yer? I was angry before any of yer were born,' said Priestley, which finished things off for Waterhouse and his friend and collaborator from Leeds, the equally clear-eyed Willis Hall. Both were well aware that anger had no part in their daily routine in London or their future plans for writing. Indeed, as Waterhouse writes in his memoir *Streets Ahead*, they were deeply content to sit around in hotel lounges ordering drinks which others paid for and discussing royalties. 'We did not want to go on writing about the north for the rest of our careers, particularly because we no longer lived there and young regional writers were coming up who knew far more about the current scene than we did,' he says. Certainly, Waterhouse returned to the gaslight, tram and cobble era in his newspaper columns, and brilliantly in his first volume of autobiography. But he never suggested that they represented the north today. On the contrary, much of his vigour when discussing the topic stemmed from his regret that they didn't.

To its credit and theirs, the north has continued to nurture outstanding writers, but with this difference: they have not followed Waterhouse's lead and their work is regularly at odds with the reality of their lives. Alan Bennett's most powerful northern images are those of a dysfunctional childhood and the overheard eccentricities of the elderly of the north (and not just the north; he also wrote about his lady in her van at his London home). But there! He has a London home, this most northern of northerners, and not only that, but his northern home is in an idyllic, even twee, village in the Dales, the tea shop capital of Clapham. His friend Russell Harty lived just down the road when he taught English and drama at a centre of northern privilege, Giggleswick public school. Its name may forever doom it to rank below Ampleforth or Stonyhurst but it is in exactly the same business: giving an excellent but very expensive education to the children of the well off.

The same is true of Simon Beaufoy, who comes from comfy Cross Hills, the home of the opulent preparatory school Malsis, where he was a pupil and his father taught English. To spell this out is not to make any adverse reflection on him and I am as enthusiastic about *Slumdog Millionaire* as the Oscar judges were. But it is to say that Beaufoy's own northern world neither was nor is the same as that which he portrayed in his first famous film *The Full Monty* or his second, *Brassed Off.* Yet there seems to be only one sort of north which tempts the metropolitan commissioners and critics, and it isn't that of Giggleswick or Malsis. The latter may well interest Beaufoy, however, and perhaps he will turn his attention to that side of the north and write about it. Given his track record and increasingly formidable reputation, perhaps the London critics will then nibble.

Can we hope the same of David Peace, another shining Northern star, but one who has so far shared the interest in grimness of his mentor the late Gordon Burn, the brilliant analyst of Peter Sutcliffe, Fred and Rosemary West and the Moors Murderers? After the unrelieved noir of *Red Riding*, oh for some subtlety, some interplay of light and shade. It can and does exist, for example in the book

Grandeur in stone. Manchester town hall

and film of *My Summer of Love*. This has plenty of the usual stuff, including dour characters and a backdrop of the miners' strike, but it gives generous space to beautiful countryside and a girl called Tamsin who speaks BBC English and goes to boarding school. As well as reflecting real life in general, it is also drawn from the actual experience of the book's author Helen Cross. She was brought up in a declining industrial area, but it was part of that peachy East Yorkshire town Beverley and she made friends with children from a posh family, of whom there are plenty in that part of the world. In a British Council interview, she recalled: 'They thought I was too rough for their beautiful children, but to their irritation I wheedled my way into some super parties and had lots of fun.' No whippets there, either.

You will also find an even-handed approach in the work of Lettice Cooper, even though she spent most of her life in London where her local bookshop in Hampstead offered her works as though they were salad, with a notice saying: 'Enjoy our local Lettice'. She was born in Eccles, given the middle name Ulpha after the Cumbrian town of her ancestors, and moved to Leeds when her father set up a steel and engineering firm in Hunslet, the childhood world of Hoggart, Waterhouse and Hall. The Coopers, however, lived in state at Roundhay Grange and although Lettice was a lifelong socialist, she gave the bourgeois north its due. The high-minded Liberal family in her best book, *National Provincial*, is based on the Lupton family of Leeds. Like me, I am sure that she stopped occasionally in front of the memorial in City Square's Unitarian church to members of the congregation who died in the first world war. They include no fewer than eight Lupton brothers whose sisters were left to carry the flag of civic duty. Alderman Bessie Lupton made a formidable lord mayor with the even more redoubtable Beatrice Kitson, of the locomotive-building dynasty, as her lady mayoress. She was also an imaginative and lively mistress of her large home in Roundhay, according to my mother, who as a schoolgirl helped to look after the Luptons' goats.

All right, lop-sided London views of the north are for the most part an irrelevance and best treated as such. I buy that absolutely. But sometimes their cumulative effect becomes serious and affects the way we carry on here. When my Manchester colleague David Ward retired in 2008, not a single journalist in the *Guardian's* London office applied for the vacancy. Up to a point, that was to do with family ties, mortgages and similar commitments, but not in every case. Who could blame the lambs when they were being treated to reports such as the one the Associated Press put out (from London) in February 2009 which starts: 'Board a train in London and in two hours you can be in Paris, City of Light – or in Manchester, city of

Artist Ben Johnson working at Liverpool's Walker gallery, 2008

grey skies and grit'? Oh come on. If I took you grit-collecting, we'd find more in Paris than in Manchester, if only on size grounds.

More significantly, the north spelt exile. It would surely be peripheral. It was far away from everything a young journalist holds dear and wants to report: the buzz, the people who matter, the centre of power. Such nervousness must account for the widely-leaked suggestion that three-quarters of the BBC staff due to come to Salford's Media City in 2011 don't want to leave London, in spite of exceptionally generous 'resettlement packages' (a term which makes it sound as if they are going to a convict settlement in the tundra). Well, someone has got to tell them not just how lovely it is, but how interesting and in no way a bar to professional success. I can do so with a certain amount of sympathy. I studied Ovid at school and his misery at exile to Tomi came back to me in 1987, when I came home every evening to Chiswick and my young family, and thought: have I done something terrible in applying for the *Guardian's* vacant

The Lowry and Millennium Bridge, Salford Quays

job in Leeds? It was my home town, long ago, but never Penny's or the children's. Would it be dull and cold and far away, and generally Tomi-like? No, no and no. I need not have worried at all and neither need the BBC's hesitant team.

How good it is when southerners do come. In March 2009, the civil service commission held an event at the Sage in Gateshead thanks to the admirable Janet Paraskeva, first commisioner, who rightly insisted on siting the English headquarters of the National Lottery Charities Board outside London – in Leicester – when she was in charge of that organisation. There had been a successful, similar civil service do in London and some argued that it would be cheaper and easier to repeat that, rather than 'dragging' the cabinet secretary Sir Gus O'Donnell and a bevy of other busy officials up north. In practice, Sir Gus was able to carry on as normal thanks to wonderful inventions such as the mobile phone and computer, and the civil servants of the north were pleased to see him and show their patch off. It was instructive to hear the reactions of cabinet office staff who had not previously been to Newcastle and Gateshead and gazed at the splendour of the Tyne bridges, old and new, with admiration.

But these are still an exception, in spite of the long history of attempts to even out the lopsided distribution of power and influence in Britain. Nearly 30 years ago, there was a particularly significant example. In the summer of 1981 after serious street violence in Toxteth, the then environment secretary Michael Heseltine persuaded Margaret Thatcher to allow him to decamp to Liverpool for two or three weeks to try and find out what had gone wrong. He discovered that this was something that no cabinet minister had done before, which says a lot about centralised government in Britain. So too does the attitude to his initiative of the Home Office, the government department primarily involved in dealing with the troubles. The home secretary, Willie Whitelaw, was a northern MP, indeed from the region's social and financial top drawer, but he was more jealous of his Whitehall empire than enthusiastic that the north might find a new champion. He did not go so far as to try to block his colleague, but appointed a minder. Luckily this was another northern member, Tim Raison, who was less hung-up on departmental pride and shared Heseltine's concern that something fundamental was amiss on Merseyside.

In his autobiography *Life in the Jungle*, the politician everyone nicknamed Tarzan includes a cinematic episode, depicting himself gazing out from his bivouac high in the Liver building, glass of wine in hand, as the sun sets over the Mersey. He wonders: 'What has gone wrong for this great English city?' He muses over the fact that the river still flowed grandly and the monumental Victorian buildings, proudly built to service an empire and handle the world's trade, still dominated the skyline. The cameo took place a while ago now, but it reveals much of the pith-helmeted explorer in the minister's mindset, just as there is among intrepid southerners who risk moving here today.

Heseltine was no mere muser, and his answer to his own question was spot on. He saw that local leadership had been sidelined by those holding real power – in London – and hence become demoralised and decayed. What initiative there was had passed to the faraway capital which wasn't very interested and had a myopic view of real life on the regional ground. Trade had been lost by weak management's hopeless warfare with what he calls 'constantly belligerent' trade unions. Talented Scousers had sought their fortunes elsewhere. The city had sunk into a long-term structural and economic decline.

How astonishingly different it is today. Liverpool preens itself with good reason on a triumphant year as European Capital of

Media City and the BBC will be the Lowry's neighbours

Culture 2008, spick, span and cleanly green – one of the north's most productive beehives is positioned on an inner-city roof with sweeping Mersey views. Heseltine used his clout to pioneer on Merseyside a momentous reform, which gave power and influence to Liverpool rather than a London address. Ever the showman, he invited the chairmen of the country's 15 largest financial institutions to join him on a bus tour of the city which also drew journalists out of their London comfort, as he had intended. Children appeared in gleeful hundreds as if the coach contained the Pied Piper. They collected autographs which they then sold on at school – a small sign of the entrepreneurial spirit reviving. But the more fundamental change was kept well away from the cameras. Heseltine devolved a small team from Whitehall to the Liver building to make sure that the programme of reforms was actually put into action. This was the blueprint for the Government Offices for the Regions which developed in stages until their full status was established in 1994.

The Baltic, Gateshead

They have been enormously, if quietly, important ever since in tackling the English regions' greatest enemy, metropolitan bias. With the final collapse of unelected regional assemblies in April 2009, they have been given even more clout, linking up with the regional development agencies – primarily economic development bodies, to promote the interests of the nine English regions.

When I returned to the north in 1987, I enjoyed teasing the then director of the Yorkshire and the Humber office, Jeremy Walker, by always referring to his set-up by the (officially forbidden) phrase 'the regional government office', which in many ways it was. He would have made a marvellous head of the civil service in an independent Yorkshire led politically by one of the county's many big hitters – William Hague, John Prescott or the Liberal Democrats' Phil Willis – but we were not supposed to go that far. Talented and energetic regional directors such as Walker were at risk if their devolving of real decision making attracted too much attention. Devolution was not Conservative policy under Thatcher and John Major, except by stealth, because it was thought to be associated by the public with extra bureaucracy and more public spending.

That thinking proved to be correct when the Conservative era finally closed in 1997 and a new dawn began with New Labour. Unfortunately, it was not new when its rays fell on the structural problem of centralised thinking, which had always threatened Heseltine's initiative and required its development to proceed discreetly. Prescott was permitted to go ahead with promoting an emasculated form of elected regional government, but there was an absolute lack of enthusiasm from the real powerbrokers of the new age, Blair, Brown, Mandelson and Campbell (for all that one of the latter's aunties played bridge every week in Bawtry, South Yorkshire, with a granny of William Hague). Depending on your taste in metaphor, Prescott was either given a few old toys in an unwanted corner of the nursery, or hung out to dry. The 'government' which he offered the regions through pallid elected assemblies was no such thing, and the voters knew it. When the chippiest of the three northern regions, the north itself (which actually embraces just the north-east and Cumbria), rejected his proposals by 78-22 per cent in a referendum in 2004, devolution of directly elected power to the regions was mothballed and has remained so.

But it would not be day-dreaming to suggest that, like the Scottish Parliament which did a phoenix act 20 years after its promoters' referendum failure in 1979, the hope of genuine English regional government may one day be revived. In the meanwhile, we retain the benign inheritance from Heseltine and his colleagues of the regional structure, which is invaluable even without a democratic, directly elected element. It is not a matter of interest only to dusty constitutional theorists, but of day-to-day practical use. A regional forum provides an alternative place to London for the many movers and shakers in the north to meet. More local power has been one of the loudest of the shouts for institutional political reform in the wake of the Parliamentary expenses furore.

In all three northern regions the unelected assemblies dismantled in 2009 had started to prove this point. They were made up of appointees from local councils, churches, universities and the like who had no real power, but they provided a focus which will be missed. Much greater potential, however, lies in the regional development agencies which have now teamed up with the government offices to speak out for us. They have decent spending money, hefty budgets of many millions annually, another Prescott legacy. Like the vanished assemblies, they are appointed rather than elected and that has made them vulnerable to scorn, particularly from the media, but they deserve better. They also bring together representatives from thriving regional institutions which have largely been immune from the 'second-rate to London' malaise. The universities, the great hospitals and the churches are all examples and all have influence on the development agencies. The agencies' meetings provide interest and exercise power in a way that demands attention from the media and makes them worth journalists' time. It is no coincidence that the reduction of other such potent forums – for example, the old and much more powerful councils – has been mirrored by a decline in the circulation and resources of local newspapers.

The agencies also have the potential to go beyond the currently hit-and-miss connections between the regions' big political beasts and the northern doorstep which they supposedly represent. In 2007, the cabinet's married couple Yvette Cooper and Ed Balls were planning an extension to their kitchen in Wakefield, where they are MPs for the neighbouring constituencies of Pontefract & Castleford and Normanton. They wanted an architect and like many others in their position, emailed the Royal Institute of British Architects for a list of local recommendations. As a result, they found the sparky and talkative Irena Bauman of Bauman Lyons in their kitchen, showering them with ideas not only about the extension but the failings of architecture and local government nationwide. Irena is based in Leeds but examines at Sheffield University and has many national and international links, reinforced in 2008 by her stimulating book *How to Be a Happy Architect*. She has the regional Royal Institute of British Architects and the Yorkshire Assembly structure to help her network, but genuinely devolved government would be far more potent. Chance would then play a less prominent role in the fruitful meeting of the likes of her and big political players such as Cooper and Balls.

Regional cohesion was also crucial when Boeing decided to build a research institution between Rotherham and Sheffield in 2001, not only because of the expertise there in highly specialised steel, but because Sheffield University and the regional development agency Yorkshire Forward drew the parties' attention to one another and helped bring them together. Liverpool's School of Tropical Medicine won $50 million from Bill Gates for the same reason, an echo of the past. In 1898, Joseph Chamberlain wanted more doctors for the British Empire and won cabinet approval for two medical schools to train them. Although always associated with Birmingham, where he had earlier been a regional leader of the finest sort, Chamberlain wanted both schools to be in London, for the usual reasons of convenience for important people and supposed saving on train fares (as if specialists visiting London from the regions travelled free and had ample spare time). He was thwarted and the London School of Hygiene and Tropical Medicine was joined by a Liverpool one rather than a second London site, only because of regional clout. The magnate Alfred Lewis Jones, head of the Elder Dempster shipping line in what was then the country's main port, not only lobbied Joe robustly but offered his own cash, like Gates. Liverpool city council in those days had powers equal to or greater than a modern regional development agency, and so the battle was won.

Another medical triumph through regional self-confidence involves the artificial joint which many of us have, or will eventually need, in one or both of our hips. This marvellous invention was the work of Sir John Charnley – not of London, but of Wrightington hospital near Wigan (and earlier, a childhood and schooling in Bury and university in Manchester). London doctors had to go to him for the training with his prosthesis on which he insisted, not the other way round. He would not budge and so they did. The socket component

The old grumbler, JB Priestley

of his revolutionary joint was also a piece of serendipity. Charnley's hunt for a suitable material was solved by a young medical engineer at Wrightington, Harry Craven, who had come from the Metal Box Company in Bradford and saw the potential in the previously little-known compound high-performance polyethylene when a sample was offered to him by a salesman from High Density Plastics, based just up the road on the Yorkshire border at Todmorden.

Experts going out from London to the regions to be trained is not the usual relationship. At the centre of the centralisers' thinking was reluctance to tolerate rival outstations of power which, however subordinate in theory, begin to show a powerful gravity of their own. Even the most enlightened organisations succumb to this paranoia. Look at the record of the BBC to see how a superbly-intentioned and sometimes aggressively devolving body is vulnerable to the

Michael Heseltine and his posse in Croxteth, Liverpool, 1981

problem. For all the genuine Reithian mission to serve the whole
country which has marked the corporation throughout its history,
from the opening of the Droitwich transmitter up to the imminent
launch of Media City on Salford Quays, internally London finds
it hard to let go. In the mid-1960s, when the BBC brought a new
phenomenon to Leeds called local radio, it was led by the wily and,
to his staff, charismatic BBC operator Phil Sidey. He and his team
overcame local reluctance to contribute through the rates for the new
experiment and downright hostility from other local media which
felt that the newcomer was competition unfairly subsidised by tax.
The *Yorkshire Post* and *Evening Post* were so hostile that the only way
Sidey could get his station mentioned in their pages was to buy a
greyhound and race it under the name of Radio Leeds. Needless
to say, this brought him a problem from a much more dangerous
quarter than the papers: his own superiors.

Sidey had paid for the dog out of his own pocket but he couldn't
resist betting on its first race as well. After it streaked home first,

merriment spread round the office and inevitably reached London, and before the day was out, the phone on Sidey's desk rang. 'There's a ridiculous story going round here that you are betting on dogs to raise money for Radio Leeds,' said the voice of one of the executives in Portland Place whose job was to keep an eye on Sidey and the other fledgling BBC local radio stations. 'I need not tell you that our friends in parliament would hardly be able to defend dog-racing for …' At that point Sidey cut in and explained, but his life as station manager was a constant battle against London fears that he would misuse what little power had been surrendered to him, all the more so because he was 200 miles from HQ and therefore, relatively speaking, out of sight.

He even lost a battle against having hat pegs on his office door; centralised BBC protocol required that a manager of his status should have three. But behind all the fun and games which made Radio Leeds so appealing, was the serious issue of the centre tugging all the time at a short leash. In the end, in Sidey's view, this dished the original ideals behind local broadcasting, although his successors at Radio Leeds and the BBC's other local stations remain bright lights in the dimming world of regional media. Although not in themselves places where anyone goes who wants to exercise influence and power immediately, they remain stepping stones to the top. One of Sidey's successors at Radio Leeds was Mark Byford, now deputy director general of the BBC.

It was the same in the disastrous quarrels which brought an end to the heyday of Granada TV in the north-west in January 1992. That was when David Plowright was sacked as head of the Granada Group's TV division, based in Manchester, a city on which the station showered awards and spread creative lustre. Plowright was a mighty name in television but that was the problem. He fell out from the start with Gerry Robinson, the new chief executive of the whole Granada group, who was based in London. The clash became a 'him or me' for Robinson, but took place in a manner which showed how deep-rooted the inability of the centre to tolerate a powerful satellite becomes. It is the fear that gravity might shift and the centre start orbiting the satellite. It goes back to royal and baronial times.

Plowright did not help matters by treating Robinson somewhat dismissively, but the real needle came when the Londoner saw the Mancunian enthroned in his regional kingdom. When the new chief exec paid his first visit to Manchester, the day ended with a disastrous dinner in the penthouse on top of Granada TV's offices where wine flowed and everyone went on about the glorious programmes the station had made. Ray Fitzwalter, then head of Granada's *World in Action*, says that Robinson 'saw Plowright, at the head of the table, as a medieval baron holding court.' On such independent-minded spirits, the tactful as well as those who stray unwisely towards contemptuousness as Plowright did, the centre's axe falls.

It is much less likely to fall in the north, however, if the centre is here. Fitzwalter is a particularly trustworthy guide to the Granada tragedy because he made his name as a journalist in Bradford, not Fleet Street. *Private Eye* picked up on a detailed analysis he wrote for the *Bradford Telegraph & Argus* in 1969 which began the collapse of the architect John Poulson's corrupt empire. Together with other investigative pieces, it won Fitzwalter the award of young journalist of the year. A similar, local base remains a journalistic advantage, but it is also the great virtue, on a far larger scale of northern-based companies such as Morrison Supermarkets. But no one should underestimate the dogged, brutal and never-ending battle which is faced by large enterprises which keep their corporate headquarters away from London. It needed all the obstinacy of Sir Ken Morrison to ride the waves of mockery, abuse and cynicism from the capital when his company had indigestion (of the most predictable kind) after swallowing Safeway in 2004. Financial journalists in London were all but unanimous that this deeply-provincial upstart had bitten off far more than it could chew.

They were wrong. Morrisons was not dependent only on northern loyalty, powerful though this is. One of my happiest northern moments was when I was mid-shop in Eccleshill Morrisons at Bradford and the tannoy interrupted the firm's terrible jingle, 'More reasons to shop at More-eezons', to announce a special offer on dripping. Jolly, yes, but don't doubt the extreme efficiency of the machine behind the business. I have family employed there, which leaves me in no doubt about the emphasis on cost-consciousness and hard work. Even a teenage niece gave evidence of the Morrisons Experience, when she was put on the tills on account of what the supervisor called with understatement her 'bubbly personality.' She caught the work ethic and not just because Sir Ken paid unannounced visits to the Guiseley store where she was bubbling, as he did to all his other branches, to check sell-by dates and make sure the best side of the purple-sprouting was showing. She got the buzz of selling, chatting, helping and meeting people's needs, even if in one case they consisted inexplicably of 80 cans of baked beans and nothing else, once a week.

The company has recovered since the Safeways takeover, and although it has brought in new blood, its headquarters remain firmly in Bradford – Gain Lane is a sacred address for northern business partisans, just as the Rowntree estate in York is for those who want to maintain a big-hitting charitable sector well away from London. It was from Bradford in early 2009 that the company, armed with sales up by eight per cent and pre-tax profits of £655 million on turnover of £14.5 billion, announced a swath of new shops in the south. It

Graham Ibbeson's marchers form the 'Spirit of Jarrow'

is down there that Morrisons has shown that a northern economic invasion of the south can work, against all the prevailing assumptions and trends. The 2008-9 sales rise was 18 per cent in London and 11 per cent over the whole of the south. When cynics claimed that southerners would shun the invader under the impression that it was another cut-price Netto, Sir Ken responded: 'Some southern shoppers like to think they're sophisticated, don't they? But they're not. There's not so much difference. They say poor people need a bargain. Well, wealthy people appreciate one.' He was right, even if he seemed to slide briefly into another false assumption: that southern shoppers are rich and northern ones poor.

Morrison is not an obviously charismatic figure, but his reticence and focus on the work is part of his appeal on home ground. He encourages artwork at his outlets, including a sculpture of the Jarrow hunger marchers by Graham Ibbeson at the Jarrow branch, but gets more plaudits for including a clock tower on almost all the stores, and making sure the four faces tell the same, and correct time. He wasn't exactly doted on as a child, but was the only boy in his family with five older sisters, and went to Bradford grammar school in its most meritocratic, direct-grant heyday (alumni from the same period in its history included Denis Healey and the late TUC secretary general Vic Feather). At the age of nine, he was checking eggs for freshness at his father's network of market stalls. Apart from national service in the Royal Army Ordnance Corps, which itself was an additional lesson in the challenges of supply, he has worked only in the business which he turned into a supermarket chain. He took over when his father fell ill in 1952, and led the enormous expansion at a slow but steady pace. He put his own family into the business; I met his daughter on the checkout at Yeadon years ago, but he didn't mind when his wife admitted shopping in Ripon Sainsbury's rather than the company's local branch. He plays the bluff northerner, to the deep-seated pleasure of small and mostly northern shareholders at the annual meeting, but he also believes in a lot of the script because – like retailing – it is what he knows and understands backwards. He also understands history, and the lessons it has for caution about letting power slip south.

Look what has happened to the debris of mighty Granada at Yorkshire Television when 600 staff were sacked and the main studios mothballed in March 2009. Look what happened many years earlier to the Lancashire Steam Motor Company, the forerunner of British Leyland, when it decided to expand and turned to London for extra capital instead of Lancashire. The company had done very well in the hands of the Spurrier family who set it up in Leyland near Preston, for all that they were a little unworldly. One of the directors had previously worked as a cowboy in the American West and another as a vicar. But in 1918 they bowed to the City of London's terms for a loan by agreeing to take on two new board members from the Square Mile. One was a man called Bevan, an apparently successful director of the City Equitable Fire Insurance company, who nonetheless went bankrupt four years later. The other was Clarence Hatry who became a notorious fraud and was jailed in 1930 for issuing unauthorised stock and forging share certificates.

This is not to say that going to London will inevitably enmesh a business in the snares of the unscrupulous or criminals, although pause with me for a minute's silence in memory of the Leeds educational printers EH Arnold. They had the ill fortune and, to be frank, wisdom-bypass, of accepting the advances in the late 1970s of Robert Maxwell who skinned and gutted their assets. The crook, and the world, was later taught a lesson by another Leeds businessman, Victor Watson, who saw off a similar hostile bid for Waddington's, the famed makers of Monopoly and Cluedo, by researching Maxwell's shady dealings offshore and threatening to publicise them. Watson was of a piece with Lord Kirkham, albeit from a different background, as a public schoolboy while Kirkham is the adopted son of a miner. But both would share the joke of Kirkham's purchase of the Thomas Gainsborough picture *Peasants Going to Market* for £3.5 million, when he floated his furniture company DFS on the Stock Exchange in 1993. Being a sensible northerner, he has since bought the company back into private ownership, while retaining the picture whose value steadily accrues.

Kirkham knows his art and so does the north. Read in awe down the list of artists born here from Henry Moore through to David Hockney; working here, from Cotman through to Turner, who sat outside the pub at Kirkstall Bridge in Leeds and left many of his finest watercolours to Farnley Hall near Otley, where he was a frequent visitor. How did the *Rokeby Venus* by Velazquez come by its name? Or the Alnwick Raphael, *The Madonna of the Pinks*?

But then turn your attention to the English Arts Council, which hands out the dosh to creatives, and the Heritage Lottery Fund, which helps galleries and much else. At the time of Michael Heseltine's Pauline vision, the Arts Council had a devolved system of regional committees, not elected or picked by jury choice which would have been even better, but made up of local people who were mostly tapped in to the literary, musical, artistic and dramatic worlds. The one I knew best was Yorkshire Arts, which had dynamos on board such as Jo Habib who has since made her name as creator of FunderFinder, based in the north and the most effective guide for grant-seekers in the charitable sector. The chair was Sir Ernest Hall, a winning combination of enterprise and art personified. He understood business well enough to turn the world's largest carpet factory at Dean Clough in Halifax into a thriving mixture of business

Sir Ernest Hall says it all at Dean Clough, Halifax

and galleries. He also plays the piano to concert hall standard and has made many recordings.

While these people were in charge (and I sensed a similar feeling from a friend involved in South-West Arts), there was a real sense of regional empowerment. They did not always make the right decisions with the budget devolved to them and they caused plenty of controversy. When things are relatively localised, there is also a risk of chumminess, both actual and in terms of damaging accusations of favouritism by disappointed grantseekers who lose out. But they were ours and they knew us. They made the excellent decision to move the regional headquarters to Dewsbury, a town usually on the sidelines watching Leeds, York or Sheffield host the big regional players. They lived up to the enormous steel capital letters in the installation by Paul Bradley which run across the front of Dean Clough, the arts centre in Halifax converted from an old mill, spelling out True North.

Now we have a Yorkshire office of the Arts Council but no powerful regional committee – any more than any of the eight other English regions. They bring in the money and dispense it efficiently, but more in the proconsular way of officials in the Roman Empire. They are directed by London and it isn't the same. By contrast, the Heritage Lottery fund retains its original system of regional committees, very similar to the old Arts Council one. They are not elected or given a jury choice element, more's the pity, but appointment by open advertisement has tapped local knowledge, imagination and vigour. The fund's programme has been especially kind to the north, encouraging oral projects about the social history of humble coalfield communities as vigorously as the more obvious heritage of stately homes.

The same is true of the National Trust, whose green-welly image is entirely belied when you visit its north-east and Cumbrian offices, which are full of the sing-song accents of local people. Some of my happiest days have been spent in their company, whether learning about the trust's heroic attempts to make Herdwick sheep wool commercially viable in the Lake District, or scrambling round the amazing landscape of Cragside, the fortress built by Lord Armstrong at Rothbury. The trust has repaired the pioneering hydro-electric system that powered the magnate's enormous home. Symbolically as well as practically, it made the place blessedly independent.

8
True North

'Ever been to London, Arnold Summergill?' 'Nay, nay
be damned. That'd be no good to me.'
James Herriot, *All Things Bright and Beautiful*

We were at the tea and whispering stage of a board meeting at the West Yorkshire Playhouse, waiting for the chair Bernard Atha to get apologies and minutes under way, when the door swung open and in walked a striking sight. It was a plump man with a cheerful face, dressed in the authentic uniform of an 18th-century town crier. The board included various arty people who never wore suits, and I have always prided myself on colourful cardigans foraged from all over the world by my younger son. But this was something else again. It was also my introduction to the Morley Independents, a group of local politicians who represent a central northern characteristic at its unrefined peak.

The town of Morley means everything to them, and 'Morley' is also their synonym for not being ruled by anyone else, or at least for a state of mind which imagines this to be the case. It has a potential dark side, in that a desire for Morley independence can become

Serene 12th-century ruins of Rievaulx Abbey, North Yorkshire

secondary to giving two really vigorous fingers to everyone else, especially the town's over-mighty neighbour and in local government terms sovereign, Leeds. But that need not be the case, and in the case of councillor Terry Grayshon it definitely isn't.

He is the jolly soul who came to the Playhouse board in theatrical clothing, not to lecture us on Morley's supposed superiority in drama as in all else. OK, Helen Fielding, the creator of Bridget Jones, is from Morley and so was the Liberal prime minister Herbert Asquith. But Grayshon had arrived to take his place on the board as one of the city council's representatives and to do his bit for the whole of the city's community. This keeps him so busy that he hadn't had time to change out of the outfit he had been wearing to promote a Christmas pantomime.

I got to know him on the board, and then in more depth when I went on an assignment to find out why the British National Party had more members in the Morley and Rothwell constituency than in any other Parliamentary seat. That was fairly quickly dealt with; there are half a dozen families with extreme right wing views and they had conducted a recruitment drive among siblings, cousins and aunties etc. It wasn't a joking matter; the BNP had managed on a low poll to take one of Morley's six seats on Leeds city council the previous year. But the Morley Independents held all the others and were well equipped and eager, compared with dozy time-servers from the big parties, to drive the nasty extreme of local chauvinism out of town.

They made that very clear as we chatted in their rooms at Morley town hall, a building modelled on the Leeds one and not a lot smaller. It is an amazing assertion of civic pride for such a modestly-sized place. No one was in fancy dress this time and Grayshon and his colleagues were very serious. They told me about a local pub which featured the familiar combination of antisocial crime including drug dealing, and being a BNP haunt, and encouraged me to go and make myself a nuisance there by asking lots of questions, which I did.

Within no time I was receiving invitations to the mayor of Morley's Christmas at-home, a lovely afternoon where all the do-ers of the town were given a thank-you by Judith Elliott, another Morley Independent on Leeds city council, for helping young people, running errands for the housebound or delivering meals-on-wheels. Again it took place at the town hall which Leeds has virtually, and very sensibly, turned back into a mostly-Morley domain, retaining only a few notices as evidence that the local council services are overwhelmingly provided by Leeds, like it or not. The whole affair reminded me of another intensely local and very independent-minded northern function, which I have never attended but would much like to.

This is the Guild of Mercers, Drapers and Haberdashers' annual dinner in Richmond, another example of strong-minded northern independence, which like Morley keeps a town council going in parallel with the supposedly more important and influential layers of district and county councils. They are not to be belittled, as providers of major services from schools to street-sweeping, but the real zing in Richmond comes from its beautiful and dignified town hall. Here resides George Coates, who still carries the title of town clerk. He also carries a silver mace to council meetings whose battered top is a symbol of how independent-mindedness has survived the most dominant of centralised regimes in times past. During the civil war, when both sides roamed around the area vying for control, the mace was hidden in a barrel of sugar for the duration. In the process, its top got knocked off.

The ebullience of Richmond town council hasn't had anything knocked off; quite the reverse. When I went there to report on one of its many achievements, the award in 2008 of market town of the year by the national Academy of Urbanism, I was ushered in by Coates, a former banker with experience in Germany, to meet the Mayor, Judith Steggles, a contented incomer (long ago) from Hampshire who taught English at a local comprehensive and was previously responsible for Richmond's award-winning floral displays. She introduced me to the broken mace and a cupboardful of ancient ceremonial robes and told me about the Mercers, Drapers and Haberdashers dinner, which she had just held with the guild's master Ken Warne, who runs a remarkable general store, part Co-Op, part Harrods, at the top of the town's fine square. 'So was it just the two of you?' I asked, imagining some dusty tryst kept going for tourist reasons or just form's sake. 'Oh no, there were at least 40 there,' she replied. Tradition is a serious business in Richmond, which also has one of the world's last surviving Guilds of Fellmongers, craftsmen who separated the pelt from sheep fleeces for glovers. There's the Richmond Buildings Preservation Trust too, which in 2003 led a multimillion-pound restoration of the former station, down below the mighty Norman castle, where you can have a cappuccino and a plate of ciabata sandwiches while waiting to enjoy a film, a crafts fair or a music workshop. And all this in a town of 8,970 people.

This contemporary form of independence is democratic and involves a lot of people, but the strength which it draws from tradition is rooted in very strong-minded individuals. They were prepared to stand up against central power and could do so in the north because of the relative remoteness of their strongholds and the clout they had earned in them. The Fielden textile dynasty of Todmorden forms a textbook example. The family became rich but stayed radical and in the words of their most famous member John Fielden MP, were never shy to admit the 'common nature of the rock from which we have been hewn.' Fielden played a full part in national politics, and was rightly considered stable and solid enough by the

England's Town of the Year 2008, Richmond, North Yorkshire

governor of the Bank of England to be given £50,000 credit in 1837 (£3,644,000 today) when American banks collapsed after taking on toxic loans and the contagion brought down British ones as well, a state of affairs easy to imagine today. But when it came to a threat to Todmorden from an ill-conceived national policy designed in London on a one-fits-all basis which bore no relation to local diversity and circumstances, he was implacable. The policy in question was the new Poor Law of 1837 which had merit in areas where local poor relief was a shambles, but not in towns such as Todmorden where it was well-administered by Todmorden people and far more humane than the rigid workhouses which the law introduced. Fielden told the commons that any attempt to impose the system on his patch would be resisted adding: 'I do not mind telling you frankly, if such resistance takes place, I will lead it.' It did and he did. At one stage, constables sent from Halifax to back the hapless new administrators of the Poor Law were stripped to their pants, rolled in mud and sent back down Calderdale in a cart. Fifty special constables and a squadron of regular cavalry eventually saw the Poor Law's structure set up in theory, but in practice a compromise led to the old Tod ways continuing behind the figleaf of new names for the officials in charge. In respect of independence as a fundamental northern characteristic, the key document is an appeal from the shaken local magistrates to the government which admitted: 'The new Poor Law cannot be successfully introduced here unless the influence of Mr Fielden can by some means be overcome by the Government.' It never was.

Independence in places such as Todmorden, where the tradition remains very much alive, is not a self-serving characteristic. It is always accompanied by a progressive aim. This sounds pious and high-minded but need not be. There are plenty of cheerful ways of serving the common good. Just as Morley and Richmond are examples, so is Hesket Newmarket at the back of Skiddaw in Cumbria, where a village co-operative has saved the local brewery which is the place's glory. Thanks to their shareholding scheme, the rest of us can still enjoy Blencathra bitter, Helvellyn Gold and Catbells pale ale.

But there is an element of faith in these bold joint ventures, and even in a secular age, it draws strength from the Faith with a capital F which has marked out the north, back to the golden age of Northumbria before the Normans came. I have accentuated the positive throughout this book, in part because that was rooted in me at Methodist Sunday school in Gipton, where we were for ever 'Climbing up Sunshine Mountain', trebling out I'm H-A-P-P-Y and even getting a crack at Bing Crosby:

> *Jonah in the whale, Noah in the ark*
> *What did they do*
> *Just when everything looked so dark?*
>
> *Man, they said we'd better*
> *Accentuate the positive*
> *Eliminate the negative*
> *Latch on to the affirmative*
> *Don't mess with Mister In-Between*
>
> *You've got to spread joy up to the maximum*
> *Bring gloom down to the minimum*
> *Have faith or pandemonium*
> *Liable to walk upon the scene.*

It was fun, and better than having to stay in chapel for the sermon. We were growing up – and I now live – in a region where spirituality is part of the landscape, and a very particular sort of spirituality. Religion in the north has always been a means to get things done. Believing is a preliminary to doing and particularly to improving. This is claimed by most religions, everywhere, but the north has centuries of evidence of it being done.

I can take you through some examples on a short northern journey: visiting the Northumbrian coast to start with, where the golden age of Anglo-Saxon England has left us a wonderful, gentle legacy of saints. I like to stop the car or gaze out of the window of the train by the sea near Alnmouth and imagine a mop-haired boy, much as I once was, wading into the breakers and preaching to the seabirds and seals. Was St Cuthbert mop-haired? Did he preach to wildlife? Haven't I just talked about 'evidence'? My daydreaming is vulnerable to all these ripostes, but such stories, including Bamburgh Castle as Lancelot's Joyous Guard and Lindisfarne as the Holy Island, have been part of northern upbringings for so long that they have moulded character and become 'real' in that sense. And even dedicated atheists in the Northumberland refer to the eider duck as Cuddy's duck.

Come south a little to Whitby, and here are the ruins of St Hilda's Abbey, the scene of a great defeat for the north in AD664, a date known to most of my generation because in chants at school it came between 597 (St Augustine's arrival in Britain) and 1066. My history teacher David Gee, a Dewsbury textile engineer's son, made the Synod of Whitby memorable by translating the issue at stake – should England opt for Roman or Celtic Christianity – into a troubling domestic scene. The two churches celebrated Easter at different times and by ill chance King Oswy of Northumbria followed the Celtic rule while his wife Queen Eanfled was a Roman adherent. The dating of Easter remains a peculiar business even in the 21st century, but at the court in Bamburgh it resulted – in Gee's enjoyable image – in

Quiet canalside in Todmorden where white and red rose meet

Eanfled tucking into a massive Easter feast at one end of the castle's vast hall, while Oswy was still picking at Lenten leftovers at the other. Alas, the synod was persuaded by the eloquence of St Wilfrid and the simple, practical rule of Celtic Christians was deposed by the wealthy, ritualistic church of Rome. At the top, at least, that was the case. But among the people and in the traditions that they handed on, Celtic ways retained their power.

Inland from Whitby is a third shrine, best reached by side roads over the numinous North York Moors where old stone crosses and carved boulders reinforce the sense that religion is part of the landscape. In the village of Lastingham, a stone crypt recalls the Celtic monastery founded here by the 'Four Cs', an aide-memoire for children trying to remember the names of the saintly brothers Cedd, Chad, Celin and Cynebal. The cramped stone chamber is early Norman; nothing remains of the timber and turf-sod original, but it has the simplicity of Celtic Christian work. Across so many years, we cannot know for

Lindisfarne castle and the wild beauty of Holy Island

sure, but the stories handed down are unanimous in their accounts of modesty, frugal living and – perhaps unusually for an organised church – following their founder's instructions to give what they had to the poor. Those who consider all this to be mumbo-jumbo may nonetheless enjoy a much later example at Lastingham of practical Christianity.

In 1806 the Archdeacon of York visited the curate there, the Reverend Mr Carter, after hearing that he was supplementing his living by fishing while his wife was running the pub. The parson explained that he and his wife and their 13 children could not survive on the stipend of £20 a year. He was a skilful fishermen and the pub was a way of using the surplus on parishioners who came a long way to church and needed refreshment; with biblical echoes of the feeding of the 5,000 as Mrs Carter cooked the fish and served them to parishioners, many of whom had to travel a long way to church and who naturally requested a drink to go with the food. Carter told the archdeacon: 'I take down my violin sometimes and play them a few tunes, which gives me an opportunity of seeing that they get no more liquor than necessary for refreshment; and if the young people propose a dance, I seldom answer in the negative; nevertheless, when I announce time for return, they are ever ready to obey my commands.' That to me is a spiritual nature at its most practical, and northern, and the archdeacon seems to have agreed. Both pub and Mr Carter stayed on.

The rootedness of religion in the north became political in a much wider sense with the foundation of the famous monastic settlements: St Bees, Shap, Jarrow, Lancaster, Fountains, Rievaulx. There are scores of them and they were fundamental to one of the great northern risings against the centre, the Pilgrimage of Grace. Robert Aske and the 30,000 men he assembled at Doncaster in 1536 made no separation between the religious faith which they saw threatened by royal moves against the monasteries, and maintaining the vigour of ordinary community life. All these years later, it is remarkable how many strands of that great convulsion remain in the north. Villages such as Egton Bridge are bastions of Catholicism because the 'old faith' was never persecuted out of them. The pub in Osmotherly is the only one in the country called 'The Catherine of Aragon', whose cause as Henry VIII's wronged wife the pilgrimage supported; yet there are dozens with the name she was given by Henry's partisans, 'The Elephant & Castle', in mockery of her title as the Infanta of Castille. The restored Catholic church, not surprisingly, has two of its intellectual powerhouses in the north at Ampleforth and Stonyhurst colleges. When I met the Eton teachers living in North Yorkshire, described in Chapter 2, I suggested one of those swaps which happen on TV reality shows, between Eton and Ampleforth's equally grand campuses. But the Catholics understandably prefer it up here.

The outsider status of Catholics after the Reformation was shared by the dissenting and nonconformist churches, and these too have been central to the spiritual character of the north. Wesley was born in Epworth. The *Manchester Guardian* was founded by a Unitarian cabal. The inherently rebellious, independent-minded spirit of noncomformity chimed precisely with the peripheral and outcast nature of the northern regions after the Stuart restoration built on the footings of Henry VIII's centralised power. A circle was completed by the exclusion of nonconformists from universities and much of political and social life; the urge to make, to do and to improve naturally turned to business and manufacturing, with momentous consequences. Not just for the north; the influence of men such as Joseph Priestley and Josiah Wedgwood became famous in Birmingham, the Black Country and the Potteries, and nonconformism held huge appeal for the working classes everywhere

Lindisfarne priory, monument to Northumbria's golden age

in England. But dissent and manufacturing marched together across the north.

Come now to another shrine, Swarthmoor Hall to the north of Morecambe Bay, which became the powerhouse of a man who is dear to me. How could he not be, when his instruction to those who thought like him was: 'Walk cheerfully over the world, answering that of God in every one.' If we substitute 'good' for 'God', non-believers can join in (especially, I hope, to spread the word among faltering, gloomy northerners, enjoyers of victim status and those who want Haworth parsonage to be a brown study). The hall was the home of the Fell family, the most influential supporters of George Fox, founder of the Society of Friends. Judge William Fell was vice-chancellor of the Duchy of Lancaster and on more than one occasion saved Fox from prison through his knowledge of legal technicalities. Margaret Fell was an early member of the Quakers, as the Friends are usually called and, after her husband's death, she married Fox.

The base they provided prompted Thomas Burroughs to rhapsodise: 'O thou north of England, whom art counted as desolate and barren, and reckoned the least of the nations, yet out of thee did the branch spring and the star rise which gave light unto all the regions round about.' That light includes the enormous past influence of the Pease family and other Quakers in Darlington, which touched so wide a nerve that the local football team are nicknamed the Quakers to this day. It lit the Cadbury touch-paper in Birmingham, where the chocolatier-turned-newspaper magnate George Cadbury introduced his *Daily News* in 1911 in terms which might startle the media today.

'I desire in founding the *Daily News* that it may be of service in bringing the ethical teaching of Jesus Christ to bear upon national questions, and in promoting national righteousness, for example that the Sermon on the Mount, especially the Beatitudes should take the place of imperialism.' Listen to the echoes across the English regions and especially in the north: WT Stead, the campaigning editor of the Quaker-funded *Northern Echo* in Darlington, who died in the *Titanic* disaster: 'What a pulpit the editor mounts daily! And from what a Bible he can choose his text – the open volume of the world.' The *Guardian's* own CP Scott in Manchester: 'I regard the figure of Jesus Christ as a moral ideal shining with divine brightness, and to approach that ideal and help others approach it is the chief aim of my life.'

These people carried their constituencies with them; they all had crackingly large funerals with long processions through bare-headed crowds, admittedly in the days before TV and the internet. Quakerism fits exactly into the northern tradition begun with the Celtic saints and later passed to secular ones such as Jabez Tunnicliff, founder of the Band of Hope and a man who made the late 19th-century campaign against drunkenness a rousing, populist affair, full of fun. Or the Rev Charles Jenkinson, the socialist chairman of Leeds housing committee in the 1920s and 30s, who rid the city of its remaining slums. It continues today, I think, in the person of John Sentamu, the Archbishop of York, who is firm and sometimes fierce but above all a do-er, and has walked cheerfully on behalf of the Church of England no end. Although his is the established church and might be suspected of opposition to dissenters and radicals, in the north this was not necessarily so. When wealthy manufacturers and the nonconformists backslid, becoming an establishment themselves and turning a blind eye to millworkers' conditions, it was an Anglican who led the charge for change. Richard Oastler denounced slavery in the mills at the same time as his fellow northern Anglican, William Wilberforce, was rooting it out overseas.

The clifftop abbey in St Hilda's Whitby

York is the last stop on my spiritual tour; but not the minster or Bishopthorpe Palace; instead, a graveyard in the grounds of The Mount psychiatric hospital where a horseshoe-shaped stone – one among rows of identical others – is engraved with the simple memorial: 'Joseph Rowntree, 24th of the Second month 1925'. The refusal to use the 'pagan' name of February marks the grave as Quaker, although there will be few readers who do not associate the name of Rowntree with Quakerism. Chocolate runs in the faith – the Frys of Somerset and Cadburys of Bournville were Friends too – but more importantly, so do good works.

I have frequently described the Homestead in York, the base of the three great Rowntree trusts, as a sacred grove. For any adult involved in radical politics, the third (charitable) sector or simply trying to improve the world, it has the magic that Lindisfarne or Bamburgh can hold for a child. From here, trustees carry out the wishes that Joseph Rowntree famously expressed in the founding deeds of his trusts: that they should 'search out the underlying causes of weakness or evil in the community, rather than remedy their more superficial manifestations.' The sentiment is not exclusively a northern one, but the expectation of dogged, thorough and often unfashionable or unpopular hard work is most commonly associated with the north. And so is the fact that this heavy burden can be shouldered lightly. My father was an often mischievous Rowntree trustee, who once took it on himself to attack the award of a knighthood to the head of the chocolate firm at the time, Donald Barron, as a prize 'for rotting children's teeth.' He was given to understand soon afterwards that Sir Donald would not wish to have lunch with trustees before their next meeting if my father was there; so he and his fellow imp on the trust, Jo Grimond, had a sausage sandwich at York railway station while the other celestial beings tucked in at the Homestead.

While all this was going on, events were taking place thousands of miles away which were to illustrate another virtue. As described in Chapter 6, the north has a record of immigration second only to London's, and I was lucky to be involved in a small and characteristic part of it. In 1972, the same year Barron was knighted, the Ugandan tyrant Idi Amin expelled some 80,000 Asian-origin fellow-citizens. Among the 30,000 who made their way to Britain was a mother of four young children, Sara Majothi, who by chance had dreamed as a little girl of working in a chocolate factory. All those years later, her dream was to come true, although not remotely in the way she had imagined. Harried halfway across the world and then crammed into a resettlement camp in a disused RAF base, she and her husband Yusuf and the children were finally taken in by a family in Leeds. That family was mine. My sisters and brother and I were away at university most of the time, so our rooms were spare. My parents saw appeals for help and decided to join what the Uganda resettlement board later called, accurately, 'a voluntary effort extended with a willingness and on a scale not seen since the second world war'. The Majothis, who had enjoyed a farm, estate and flour-milling business in Uganda, arrived on our doorstep with a suitcase each and the balance of £55, all the cash they had been allowed to take with them.

None of us, Wainwrights nor Majothis, have forgotten the six months' stay, which started with the children being so restrained and polite at their first, welcoming supper ('Don't show me up, children, don't eat too much, don't gobble,' Sara told them beforehand) that they crept down after midnight to open and eat a tin of baked beans, cold. 'We all remember those beans,' says Naseem, the second daughter who is now 48, as she prepares food at the family's takeaway in York. Food was a constant theme. The youngest son Shiraz's first encounter with a brussels sprout at Christmas dinner sticks in the

Whitby harbour, where James Cook learned his trade

memory, along with Yusuf patting his tummy after the same meal and announcing: 'I am fed up.' His nephew, visiting from Leicester where some of the 43 other members of the extended Majothi family had ended up, joined in by courteously thanking my parents 'for giving my uncle a good shed'.

Yusuf had the immigrant's overwhelming need to find work. Within a month, he had drawn up a scheme to sell chickens door-to-door in Headingley with my father, whom, as chairman of the Liberal party at the time and a former MP, he considered a useful name. 'You are my atom bomb,' was the way he put it. Dad managed to be enthusiastic but evasive, a combination which he also needed to deploy on constant gifts of food from Sara. The most frequent were chapatis, lovely ones but my father did not like them and was also trying to keep his weight down. He hid them in a drawer.

Everyone learned and benefited and we have kept up for the 33 years since; I was almost knocked flat by a huge slap on the back at my father's funeral; turning round, it was Yusuf with warmth, sorrow and pleasure at seeing the rest of us again, fighting for control of his large, expressive face.

We were only a small part of the northern package that helped the Majothis find their feet. Leeds employment exchange, York housing department, the villagers of Stockton-on-the-Forest and, yes, the chocolate factory all played their part. The family were rehoused at Stockton and arrived to find their semi decorated in advance by the village. They have never forgotten their new neighbours, especially the Hall family, who farm at Stockton and smile from a collage of photographs behind the counter at the takeaway.

'Mrs Hall was a grandmother to us,' says Sara, whose initial loneliness was eased by the older woman's kindness. The Halls backed her stoutly when she applied to Rowntree's, which had already taken

Northerners triumphant. Ringo, John, Paul and George

Yusuf on. 'The old man saw my applications and said: "What are these forms? My wife is not going out to work." But I did. I told him: "Old man, it is good that God did not make more than one of you." I also got the bus there on my own.'

So it was that Sara Majothi realised her girlish dream, and there was a touching episode when she told her new workmates in her still-halting English about the coincidence. One of the dream's recurring episodes involved her plunging her arms up to the elbows into piles of the brightly coloured sweets 'and, you know, just throwing them about'. Someone mentioned it to a manager; they had plenty of reject Smarties at the factory, and so, Willy Wonka-like, they let her do it.

While they found their feet, the Majothis were supported by their new neighbours. Once they were stable, the benefits went equally and in the end more, the other way. The Symryn takeaway, named after family members' initials, is a terrific place for a curry if you are in York and I am trying to use my *Guardian* influence to get Dr

John Sentamu, Archbishop of York

Sentamu, also a Ugandan and a fellow-victim of Idi Amin, to pick up a meal there. Faith is something they share; the Majothis are devout Muslims like many other new northerners from East Africa and the Indian sub-continent. Islam is an austere faith with simple practices and a localised hierarchy which reflects that of many nonconformists. Our neighbours returned from a holiday in rural Turkey some years ago and told us how similar they found the buildings and atmosphere in the village mosques to the Methodist chapels we have round here. We went a couple of summers later and saw what they meant.

Austerity is a potentially misleading word for the effects of northern faith, however. My family's connections with the Majothis were marked not by a sense of obligation or duty, but by fun. There are many ways of expressing this in the wider sense, and one of the characteristics of the north is its long roll-call of professional funsters. Has any other part of Britain produced so many comedians?

As children, we fell off our seats with laughter at Jimmy Clitheroe, the little clown at the Christmas pantomime who was no bigger than us, but being 30 years older could make much better jokes. Our cosmopolitan world was enhanced by Charlie Williams, the first black comedian to earn major TV success, who had us all mimicking 'me old flower.' He was from Royston, a pit village near Barnsley, where his father settled and set up a horse and cart grocery, after enlisting in the Royal Engineers from Barbados during the first world war. Williams was a courageous model for brilliant successors such as Lenny Henry, and had an ace response to hecklers during the era of Enoch Powell: 'If you don't shut up, I'll come and move in next door to you.' He knew all about racism, but also about integrating. As a centre-half for Doncaster Rovers, he came up with a pitch-perfect description of his role: 'I were never a fancy player, but I could stop them buggers as was.'

Ugandans like the Majothi family arrive in 1973

Yes, there was Bernard Manning too. But let's tag him as a footnote, and concentrate on Eric Morecambe from Morecambe, and Ernie Wise, another of the glorious sons and daughters of Morley. And see how the suburban virtues of Lytham St Annes inspired the surrealism of Les Dawson, whose statue now looks out, baffled as ever, at the ornamental gardens by the resort's pier. Anyone who could start a gag with 'I was vouchsafed this vision by a pockmarked Lascar in the arms of a frump in a Huddersfield bordello …' was taking something special from the rock out of which he was hewn. His spirit lives on in *The League of Gentlemen* and Royston Vasey.

It did not take much to prompt a northern comedian to burst into song, and music is another essential part of the north. Like humour, it has connections to faith, most pithily expressed in the Methodist Hymn Book introduction's first sentence 'Methodism was born in song.' One of the abiding images of the north is the choral society. Along with my neighbours, I will do anything for a place in the audience at one of December's great renditions of *Messiah*, although I have never yet succeeded in getting a ticket to the greatest of them all, at Huddersfield town hall. The combination of the Huddersfield Choral Society and the Hallé under Sir Malcolm Sargent was the stuff of legend when I was small, but neither institution remotely belongs to that past. The Hallé is at the peak of its powers in 2009 and Huddersfield resounds to a marvellous variety of musical sounds. The choral society thrives mightily, but as noted in Chapter 7, the town is also the home of Britain's most highly-rated contemporary music festival. A couple of years ago, I had a great time there listening to the Vienna Vegetable Orchestra playing on recorders made of carrots, red pepper trumpets and violins strung from leeks, all of them carved freshly just before the concert. The only pity was that we were denied the soup, which the musicians normally make for the audience after each event, for health and safety reasons.

Huddersfield is also the home of the Longwood Sing, a mass gathering of anyone and everyone, including the tone deaf such as myself, who want to enjoy the fresh air and views from Nab End Tower while belting out hymns. The bellringers at St Mark the Evangelist help along and you will more than likely find a brass band nearby. They are everywhere in the north, of course, and when the Lottery distributors started funding them in the late 1990s, the British brass instrument manufacturers couldn't cope with demand, and orders had to be placed all over Europe. I have a retirement fantasy about learning to play the trumpet, so that I can perform 'The Trumpet Shall Sound' from *The Messiah*, with its thrilling advance up the scale. But by that time, my teeth may make the undertaking too dangerous. I remember interviewing a very young cornet player who had chafed at the delay in admitting him until he had lost all his milk teeth, in case he blew one loose and choked. Once you reach the stage of false teeth, the same caution is wise.

Longwood is known as the mother of all sings but there are many of them, often associated with hilltops where Easter choral services take place at sunrise across the north, from Otley Chevin to Teggs Nose quarry above Macclesfield. This is a bit early for me, but I have taken part in the unique pub carols which take place in December at a small number of villages round Sheffield. If you want to sing your way through some 15 subtly different versions of 'While Shepherds Watched', this is the place to be. The tradition dates from the rise of a centralised musical tradition in the Anglican church, which left no place for local versions of hymns and carols other than the pub, much in the way that Thomas Hardy's church orchestras were expelled by the installation of organs. The sessions have been revived and developed as a fascinating form of communal singing, which reaches high standards but nonetheless welcomes outside visitors. A pubful of singers in full voice is quite a sight and it is worth reading the online advice of the Yorkshire Folk Arts society. For example: 'Moving to the bar and back can be extremely difficult, as can visiting the toilet'. I can vouch for that, although the carolers have an excellent system of passing empty glasses from hand to hand to the bar for refilling, and then back, with instructions and reminders sometimes sung between 'Hark! Hark!' or 'Hail, Shining Morn!'

I would like to be able to sing properly, like Penny, who belongs to one of our (many) local choirs. At one of her recent concerts, I confided my trumpet-learning hopes to the gentleman next to me in the audience. He advised me to try the ukulele instead. It is certainly northern enough, thanks to George Formby of Pembleton, near Wigan, and also apparently quite easy to master. But on reflection, the instrument I would most like to have a go at is that final northern wonder, the musical stones of Skiddaw.

They were the work of a stonemason from Keswick, Joseph Richardson, who was an enthus iastic musician in the Longwood Sing and Sheffield carols tradition. As a young man in the early 1800s, he noticed that the rocks he was cutting or carving produced different musical notes, and in due course he discovered that the hornfels outcrops of Skiddaw, Keswick's own mountain and the fourth highest peak in England at 3,054ft (931 metres), gave the truest sounds. Thus began the construction of what was in effect a stone xylophone, framed in mahogany and containing eight octave sets made of stone. In 1840, after months of practising, Richardson and his sons embarked on a trial tour of concerts in northern towns which was so wildly popular that they did not come back to Keswick for three years.

Carols on a 'Singing Special' train from Sheffield to the Peak

Their lithophone, as it became known, was then invited to London and its renditions of increasingly complicated music, including works by Handel, Mozart and Beethhoven, took the city by storm. It was described as creating effects from the trill of an ascending lark to the tolling of a funeral bell, and in 1848 the Richardson team, by then known popularly by the satisfactory name of the Rock Band, played in Buckingham Palace at the invitation of Queen Victoria and Prince Albert. I heard the stones played again in 2006, when the percussionist Evelyn Glennie presented a Radio 4 documentary about them. They sounded great, and they – or the sounds they make – are due to make plenty more excursions from their permanent home at Keswick Museum. A rock band, the Stones…Goodness, I am running out of pages and I have barely mentioned the Beatles, or the Hacienda, or Stone Roses, Pulp, or the Kaiser Chiefs. May I take it that the lustrous tradition of modern music in the north is too well known, and too widely recorded, for me to do more than salute in admiration here? Even the Beautiful South whose members were actually all from the north apart from Sean Welch and developed from a Hull band, the Housemartins. Singer Paul Heaton chose the new name for two reasons: in irony, because he prefers the north generally; and to force northern macho men, whom he isn't so keen on in particular, to have to say the word 'beautiful.'

If I am chided for giving such small space to rock musicians – and a story such as the Beatles' says everything I want to say about achievement in and from the north – then how much more of a sinner I am when it comes to sport. I'm sorry. I was one of those nerdy kids who was always in the last two picked when the fit ones were choosing teams. But anyway, does anyone not know about the glories of Liverpool, Manchester United, the Magpies, the Owls, Len Hutton, Giant Haystacks or – and a big hurrah for Hull – the

Morecambe and Wise. Northern comics make the world laugh

combo of Premier League football and Super League rugby at the mouth of the Humber? OK, the Tigers escaped relegation in May 2009 by a solitary point, but escaping is all that matters. Not that northern communities depend on great football teams for success and prosperity. My own home, Leeds, has proved that point.

And there is something else: a link, between the global nature and commitments of the north's great sporting teams, and my final virtue of the modern north. We are rooted, we love our communities and want to improve them, but we also go out into the world and want to discover and enjoy it.

Sometimes this can be done without leaving home. I have mentioned Thomas East and his substitution of a real visit to Palestine with one he made in his mind (qv page 172), and I enjoyed coming across a similar example near Barnsley, on the other side of the valley from the Northern College among its rhododendrons at Wentworth Castle. In the same enlightened spirit as the college, a local farmer and landowner called Alfred Octavius Elmhirst but generally known as Pom, invited the Open College of the Arts to move from London to his Tudor farmhouse at Houndhill just up the road from Arthur Scargill's house. It was a huge success. The staff loved the place, with its geese, ducks and remains of fortifications erected in the civil war, but the fascinating thing was this northern nook's connections with the outside world. The open college was founded by Michael Young, who helped to draft the radical 1945 Labour manifesto and was also instrumental in founding the Consumers' Association and the Open University. Like Elmhirst, whose family had virtually adopted him, Young was an internationalist above all else. By the time the open college moved to Houndhill, it was organizing 30 courses for

Sir Mark Elder and the Halle Orchestra in rehearsal, 2009

45,000 students and 300 tutors worldwide. This global operation was being co-ordinated, when I visited in the summer, by staff working outside in the sunshine under sunhats made from folded pages of the *Barnsley Chronicle*.

Although such virtual world travelling is increasingly practicable, thanks to the internet, the north will also continue its practice of actually sending people out into the world. If you do come to live here, your name will not be blackened if you then move on. What else could be expected of a region responsible for Wrigley's chewing gum, the work of a Saddleworth family which emigrated to the United States to make worsted, and started the gum as a gimmick to help their salesmen there? Or which produced William Scoresby, the adventurous whaler from Whitby? He first went hunting in the Arctic at the age of 11 with his father, who made a fortune out of whaling. William junior was equally excited by the hunt, but developed his interests to include mapping the Greenland coast, submitting a paper on compass anomalies in the far north to the Royal Society, serving as a curate near Whitby and marrying three times. It is only fair that such an enthusiast should be commemorated, among other things, by a crater on the moon. His voyages were also celebrated more recently by one of those northern stories of pluck against adversity that makes the transition so rapidly into film. *Captain Jack* did not enjoy the success of *The Full Monty*, *Brassed Off* or *Calendar Girls*, but Bob Hoskins did credit to both Scoresby's memory and the character of the 20th-century Whitby mariner he plays in the movie. This was Jack Lammiman, another adventurous northern roamer, who evaded marine safety officials to reach Scoresby's old whaling grounds in his ancient and leaky ship the *Helga Maria* and plant a plaque in memory of the great man. And then there was William Strickland, another sea captain who introduced the turkey from America and is

Eyes on the horizon; Captain Cook's statue in Whitby

remembered by the unique turkey lectern in the church at Boynton near Bridlington, where he rebuilt the Norman manor house with the proceeds from his brainwave into what is now Boynton Hall.

Wandering northerners in fiction compose a genre which deserves a book of its own; I keep a list as I come across them in my own reading. There are dozens but I will just mention two which particularly intrigued me, one of whom is at the centre of a puzzle which you may be able to solve. The first is the anonymous Yorkshire woman at the centre of Jorge Luis Borges' short story '*The Warrior and the Captive Maiden*', in which an Argentine government official records encountering this exile living as the wife of the chieftain of a local Indian tribe. He finds out her origins after noticing the blonde roots of her otherwise dark hair. The story is full of mystery, as to how the woman got there and what she does – and, best of all, whether her disconcerting habit of drinking the warm blood of an animal freshly killed by her warrior husband was a 19th-century Yorkshire habit or a south American Indian one.

Secondly, I sat bolt upright when the heroine of Jean Giradoux's Robinson Crusoe novel of the 1920s, *Suzanne et le Pacifique*, discovered the body of a British naval rating washed up on the island where she was marooned after winning a round-the-world cruise on a luxury liner which then sank. On his arm, says Giradoux, was a tattoo reading: 'I am a son of happy Leeds.' Looking wistfully down at the handsome but lifeless young man, Suzanne reflects on his faraway home: 'Un fils de l'heureuse Leeds, de la riche Leeds, grouillante d'épingles de tête et d'épingles à cheveux plus qu'un divan.' I translate this literally as, 'A son of happy Leeds, of rich Leeds, more alive with hatpins and hairpins than a sofa, ' but cannot fathom its actual meaning. If you can help, I will host you on a weekend tour of the north.

Finally there is Captain Cook, who always tops polls of famous northerners in history, and whose museum in Whitby, in the quayside house where he trained for the sea, is one of the pleasantest outings you can make. Its high spot for me is an account of how an elderly maidservant, who had mothered Cook during his stay, had to be taken aside and calmed down when he returned as a famous man to catch up with Yorkshire friends. 'He's very important now and won't want to be bothered,' they told her. But when she caught sight of her former charge, she forgot it all and rushed forward with a cry of 'Honey James, it be so good to see thee!'

What a lovely welcome – and it always reminds me of the one we got here, when we arrived in 1987 and met the neighbours for the first time. Where were we from? A little sheepishly, not certain of the reaction, we explained that we had been in London for the last 12 years in my case, and in Penny and the boys' for all their lives. 'Oh come in,' she said, in tones which I am certain echoed those of James Cook's old nurse and which you can expect if you move up here. 'You'll be needing a cup of tea.'

Epilogue

*'Therefore thus saith the Lord of hosts; Because ye have
not heard my words, Behold, I will send and take all the
families of the north and will bring them against this
land, and against the inhabitants thereof, and against
all these nations round about, and they will utterly
destroy them, and make them an astonishment, and
an hissing, and a perpetual desolation.'*
'Jeremiah' Chapter 25 Verse 9

In August 2009, the National Union of Sub-Editors agreed overwhelmingly, with only the Islington and Westminster branches dissenting, to ban the phrase 'Grim up north' from headlines for ever. An amendment adding 'Our Friends in the north' to the proscribed list, on the grounds that it had only ever been used in a patronising context, was also carried by a substantial majority.

The news was greeted in the sunlit cities and villages of the north with the ringing of church bells, a special gamelan concert in Hebden Bridge and community swims from the sweeps of yellow sand on either side of the Tyne, Wear, Tees, Humber, Dee, Mersey and Morecambe Bay. Music, theatre, opera and ballet productions observed a minute's silence at dozens of venues and the kitchens of master restaurateurs such as Thomas Hetherwick in Preston and Anthony Flynn in Leeds briefly – very briefly – laid aside their oyster shuckers and crème brûlée torches.

Well, not quite yet. But may that glorious day be soon in coming. And may the fifth column of northern whingers who maintain the dreary mindset of victimhood, pass peacefully to a long and well-earned period of silence, or go for improving walks. I know there is a downside to life up here, just as there is everywhere in the world. But we really don't need to go on about it.

I have gone on to the opposite extreme, I know. Guilty as charged. But I've just sent an internet link to my publisher Lisa Darnell, the head of Guardian Books, of a story published only hours before I started this epilogue. It's by me admittedly, but I picked it up from the *Sunday Times* which in turn got it from a number of internet sites (so the circle, as ever, turns). Here's the headline: Upbeat memoirs of northern childhood to have sequels. And here's the subject: the autobiographies of Peter Kay and Paul O'Grady (Lily Savage) about their childhood and youth in Bolton and Liverpool were the best-selling hardbacks in the UK in 2006 and 2008 respectively, so the publishers want more.

The era of Misery Memoirs is over, they say – sales of ghastly parents and living in a paper bag were down by 35 per cent in 2008-9. Hooray! Let's extend that trend to the whole, wider genre of Misery north. I do not expect the world to buy 750,000 copies of this (as per Kay's *The Sound of Laughter*), or even 600,000 (the tally for O'Grady's *At My Mother's Knee – and Other Low Joints*), but give it your best shot. I will meanwhile pre-empt any critic who might be tempted to re-entitle this book *The Sun Shines out of the North's Arse*, with myself possibly taking the latter role. Do your worst, because it does.

Index

A
accents 54–7, 88–90, 194
Afghans 185–6
African ancestry 182–3
agriculture 40
Ajeeb, Mohammed 205–6
Allerton Bywater 131, 132
Alsop, Will 76–7
ancestry 182–3
Andy Capp 26–7
Appleby horse fair 161
art 256–8
attractions 60–1
Auden, WH 178–9

B
Barnsley
Brass for Barnsley 140
industry 74–7
women in 136–7
Bauman, Irena 247
Beaufoy, Simon 236
Bede, Venerable 183–4
beef dripping 92–4
Bennett, Alan 235–6
Bewick, Thomas 172–3
black pudding 99–100
Boeing 248
book burning 189
Bradford
countryside around 154–5
immigration 193–4
Brass for Barnsley 140
Britton, Rita 74–5

Brontë family 70–1, 168, 221–2
Bruegel, Pieter 232–3
buildings
pioneering 225–8
renovation of old 67–8
Burke, Ian 49–52

C
Cadbury, George 273–4
Catholics 271–2
Chamberlain, Joseph 248
change 80–1
Charnley, Sir John 248–9
choral societies 283–4
clichés 17
Coalfields Communities Campaign 124
coal-mining industry 121, 123, 124–42
Coates, George 264
comedians 281–2
community 34
Conservative party 245
Cook, Captain 292
Cooper, Lettice 238
cosmopolitan community 71–2
crime 112–13
Crossley family 116
Crow Nest park 115
cuisine see food

D
dams 112
Danby 49–51
dark, light and 222–6
deprivation 121
Dholakia, Lord 201–2

Index of Photographers

Bibliography, further reading
and your chance to comment and debate are on

http://martinwainwright-truenorth.blogspot.com